THE LAKESIDE COMPANY
CASE STUDIES
IN AUDITING
TWELFTH EDITION

JOHN M. TRUSSEL
Dalton State College

J. DOUGLAS FRAZER
Millersville University

PEARSON

Boston   Columbus   Indianapolis   New York   San Francisco   Upper Saddle River

Amsterdam   Cape Town   Dubai   London   Madrid   Milan   Munich   Paris   Montreal   Toronto

Delhi   Mexico City   Sao Paulo   Sydney   Hong Kong   Seoul   Singapore   Taipei   Tokyo

Editor in Chief: Donna Battista
Acquisitions Editor: Stephanie Wall
Editorial Project Manager: Christina Rumbaugh
Senior Managing Editor: Cynthia Zonneveld
Production Project Manager: Carol O'Rourke
Senior Operations Supervisor: Diane Peirano
Printer/Binder: BindRite Graphics, Robbinsville

Credits and acknowledgments borrowed from other sources and reproduced, with permission, in this textbook appear on the appropriate page within text.

4 5 6 7 8 9 10 V056 13

PEARSON

ISBN 10: 0-13-013256725-3
ISBN 13: 978-0-13-256725-1

The Lakeside Company: Auditing Cases (12e)

CONTENTS

The Lakeside Company:
Auditing Cases (12e)

Overview

The Lakeside Company was conceived as a means of introducing students to the world of auditing that exists outside of a college textbook. These cases have been used at hundreds of universities and by thousands of students. Over the years, these cases have evolved to mirror both the continual changes found in the auditing profession as well as refinements in our approach to the presentation of many subjects. We believe this edition is a particularly efficient and effective educational tool. The webpage for the book, http://www.pearsonhighered.com/arens, includes audio clips, electronic working papers (templates for exercises), and links to other websites. The instructor's manual also includes solutions to discussion questions and exercises.

Few courses at any college are more interconnected with actual practice than Auditing. Many accounting majors find themselves serving as a member of a real audit team within just a few months following graduation. Textbooks have traditionally approached the subject by attempting to develop an appreciation in students for the various aspects of an audit: client acceptance, potential legal liabilities, internal control assessment, audit risks, analytical procedures, and the like. Although each of these topics can be comprehended in the abstract, understanding is frequently enhanced if students can place them within the context of an actual audit. Unfortunately, most college students do not have the opportunity to participate in an audit experience prior to graduation.

The cases in *The Lakeside Company* are intended to create a realistic view of how an auditor organizes and performs an audit examination. These cases provide a simulation that permits students to put the abstract and difficult concepts of auditing into practice. Students are guided through the phases of an audit from beginning to end. Every effort has been made to provide situations that are not particularly unusual, the kinds of problems that an auditor might face each day on the job.

Students have to perform realistic audit activities, such as:

- Analyze fraud risk factors
- Assess the implications of the Sarbanes-Oxley Act
- Perform analytical procedures
- Determine the materiality level
- Determine inherent risk
- Determine control risk

- Prepare internal control flowcharts and narratives
- Prepare and review audit documents (working papers)
- Prepare audit programs and apply audit procedures
- Perform statistical sampling procedures
- Prepare audit reports

Students are introduced to a world where decisions must be made under conditions of risk and uncertainty, client pressures, and time constraints. Although these cases cover the diverse components of an audit, their main focus is on assisting students to develop an understanding of the logic used by auditors in making a determination about a client's financial statements.

In contrast to most accounting textbooks, the questions and concerns posed by these cases rarely have set answers that are ultimately correct. We believe that in a real audit no easy answers usually exist for the many complex problems that may be encountered. Instead, the auditor must analyze each situation, consult with authoritative literature, and finally rely on professional judgment to justify the actions being taken. Students simply looking for answers and procedures to memorize may be frustrated by *The Lakeside Company*. Conversely, students who question what they are told, refuse to accept untested assertions, and enjoy the interchange of ideas about the real meaning of events, actions, and figures are often fascinated by these cases.

When *The Lakeside Company* was first developed, we wanted to create a tool that was readily adaptable to the needs of any college professor. Therefore, several characteristics of these cases should be noted.

Characteristics

- The website includes audio clips, electronic working papers (with text files in Microsoft Word and spreadsheet files in Microsoft Excel) and links to other websites. The instructor's version includes solutions to discussion questions and exercises.

- The cases can be used with any textbook. Students should consult frequently with their textbooks to help them resolve difficulties and justify their actions but the cases are not dependent on the use of any particular book.

- The cases can be used in virtually any order; each one is written as a relatively independent situation. When time is a problem, some cases may simply be omitted or not covered in their entirety. Obviously, not all professors want to approach this course in a prescribed manner. *The Lakeside Company* cases can be ordered in any way that best fits each professor's preferred presentation, although the introductory case should be assigned first.

- The cases offer an array of possible approaches: discussion questions, exercises (with related electronic working papers), and research assignments. The type of questions can be used that suit a particular professor's style. These cases were originally intended for open classroom discussion, many times like a debate.

- Students can work individually or in teams. One possibility is to divide the class into audit teams at the beginning of the semester so that the students can experience working in groups, a skill that is essential in auditing.

- *The Lakeside Company* is based on a regional public accounting firm as well as a regional nonpublic business client. Virtually all of the questions, though, relate equally to both smaller and larger firms and clients. The instructor may wish to point out differences in auditing a public company as opposed to a nonpublic one.

- Audio Clips: The website includes audio clips prepared by the "consulting partner" on the audit team (under the title "Consulting Partner Review"). The consulting partner offers additional questions that require critical thinking about the subject material of the cases. Students listen to the clips, read the material related to the clips, perform additional research, and prepare additional memos or reports.

- Electronic Working Papers (Templates): The website includes supplemental templates for the exercises that may be used as audit documentation (i.e., working papers). These templates include either word-processing or spreadsheet templates that may be used to document solutions to the exercises. The word-processing files are in Microsoft Word for Windows® version 7.0 format. The spreadsheet files are in Microsoft Excel for Windows® version 7.0 format. We find that these are excellent for creating a paperless auditing course, with assignments submitted electronically. Each exercise has a reference to the name of the template available for download from http://www.pearsonhighered.com/arens.

- The implications of Sarbanes-Oxley. Although the Lakeside Company is a privately held company, the company's management is considering the issuance of stock to the public. Thus, students are asked to address the implications of the Sarbanes-Oxley Act on both the client and the auditor.

- **New!** Additional ethics and fraud questions. Several additional questions have been added regarding both ethics and fraud. We identify questions about ethics with a logo of a scale and questions about fraud with a logo of a triangle.

- Risk Assessment Standards incorporated in cases. In March 2006 the AICPA's Auditing Standards Board issued SAS 104 to 111, eight standards relating to the assessment of risks in a financial statement audit. The Risk Assessment

Standards establish standards and provide guidance in financial statement audits for private companies concerning the auditor's assessment of the risks of material misstatements (whether caused by error or fraud) and the design and performance of audit procedures that are responsive to those risks. In addition, these Statements establish standards and provide guidance on planning and supervision, the nature of audit evidence, and evaluating whether the audit evidence affords a reasonable basis for the auditor's opinion on the financial statements under audit. The primary objective of the Statements is to enhance the auditor's application of the risk model. We have incorporated questions and references related to these standards throughout the cases.

- Assignments: Many of the questions in this book are open-ended, designed to stimulate the ability to analyze auditing problems. Often, as in a real audit, no absolutely correct answer is possible. Students must evaluate the facts and attempt to arrive at a logical conclusion or a viable course of action. To guide the analysis, students should consider consulting a standard auditing textbook, the "Statements on Auditing Standards" issued by the Auditing Standards Board, or any other relevant authoritative pronouncements produced by the AICPA.

- Research Questions: Many cases include a section called "Apply Your Research" in which students are asked to expand on a topic addressed in the case. Students should research these questions using online databases available from their libraries, such as ABInform, ProQuest, or Nexus-Lexis.

- **New!** Students are required to develop a preliminary judgment about materiality. This assignment asks students to consider quantitative and qualitative aspects of the materiality decision.

- **New!** Students are required to develop the appropriate level of inherent risk for the client as a whole. Students have to take into account a variety of information and use their judgment to determine inherent risk.

- **New!** Students are required to develop the appropriate level of control risk for a particular segment of the client's operations. Students have to use flowcharts and narratives and use their judgment to determine control risk.

Resource for Instructors

For the instructor, the website http://www.pearsonhighered.com/arens includes a solution's manual. This manual provides complete, detailed solutions to all discussion questions and exercises.

We hope that you find your experiences with *The Lakeside Company* to be both educational and enjoyable. Auditing is truly a fascinating subject to study. We have tried to capture some of our enthusiasm for this topic in these cases. The emotional approach to education is often dependent on one's perspective. For example, is determining the areas within an audit that have high inherent risk drudgery or an interesting exploration of a client company? Is estimating a warranty liability a boring mechanical procedure or a type of puzzle where all available information must be sorted through to arrive at a viable estimation of a future event? Ultimately, each student must decide whether the material is to be viewed as interesting or dull. We hope these cases will share some of our interest in auditing.

Best wishes for a great class!

John M. Trussel, Dalton State College (jtrussel@daltonstate.edu)
J. Douglas Frazer, Millersville University (Doug.Frazer@millersville.edu)

The Lakeside Company: Auditing Cases

A LOOK INSIDE A CPA FIRM

i. INTRODUCTORY CASE

The CPA firm of Abernethy and Chapman is located in the central portion of Virginia. This partnership began operations in 1979 and now employs 145 accountants out of a main office in Richmond and three branches in nearby Virginia cities. The Richmond office has 87 professionals: 10 partners, 14 managers, 21 senior, and 42 staff auditors. Eleven members of this group concentrate in tax services while another seven offer a variety of consulting services to the firm's clients. The others spend a majority of their time performing audits, other assurance services, accounting and bookkeeping services. During busy periods, individuals occasionally have to move from one area of the firm to another. Eighteen additional employees comprise the secretarial and clerical staff of the Richmond office. At present, all of the firm's audit clients are non-public companies. However, the firm is considering adding some clients that are publicly traded companies.

In hiring professionals, the firm considers only college graduates with a major in accounting and requires that each employee sit for the CPA exam within one year of employment. Once employed, all accountants in the firm must complete at least 40 hours per year of continuing education. Promotions within the firm are guided by seniority and technical competence. For example, for a staff auditor to be promoted to senior auditor, he or she must have been with the firm at least two years, must have passed the CPA exam, and must have demonstrated outstanding competence in job performance.

DeAnna Malott, a partner in the Richmond office, monitors the quality control standards and the human resource policies of the firm. One of Ms. Malott's responsibilities is to conduct training seminars for new professionals regarding the policies of the firm. Under these policies, employees must sever all financial ties to audit clients. Another of Ms. Malott's duties is to assign personnel to the various audit engagements of the firm. In making these assignments, she considers the employee's experience with the client's business, as well as his or her technical training. For audit engagements, firm policy requires the assignment of a consulting partner, as well as a partner-in-charge of the engagement. The partner-in-charge of the audit heads the engagement team, while the consulting partner advises and reviews the final work of the team.

The audit engagement team consists of a partner-in-charge, a manager, a senior auditor, and one or more staff auditors. The partner-in-charge of the engagement has the definitive responsibility for decisions made during the audit, even though he or she does not normally carry out the major activities of the audit. The manager, senior auditor, and staff auditors perform the majority of the procedures required by an audit. The assignment of an engagement team, as well as a consulting partner, is to ensure not only that audits are appropriately supervised but also that there is complete objectivity and competence in conducting each audit.

Abernethy and Chapman as a firm, and the Richmond office in particular, has experienced considerable growth over the past five years. The partners believe that a good marketing strategy and a continuing emphasis on high-quality auditing and accounting services have generated the increase in revenues. During the most recent fiscal year, the Richmond office totaled over $7,000,000 in gross revenues while earning nearly $2,000,000 in net income. Profits accruing to individual partners ranged from $150,000 to $400,000. Traditionally, 60% of the firm's income has been derived from audit engagements with tax services providing another 25% of the total. Remaining revenues are generated by assurance services other than audits (e.g., reviews), accounting and bookkeeping services (e.g., compilations), and consulting services. The partners agree that assurance services (including financial statement audits) and consulting services offer the greatest potential for expanding the firm's income and have constantly stressed the growth of these services. Public company auditing is a prospective area for growth, but it brings new risks.

At present, Abernethy and Chapman has a number of large clients in the Richmond area: a small hotel chain, a group of furniture stores, several large car dealerships, and three of the local banks. Recently, the firm decided to seek additional clients. Therefore, within the last 18 months, a series of advertisements has been published in local newspapers as well as in several prominent Virginia periodicals. In addition, a monthly newsletter describing current accounting and taxation changes is distributed to clients and local business leaders. This marketing strategy was created by a Richmond advertising agency and has stressed the theme "We Are Here to Help Your Business." The entire campaign cost the firm approximately $200,000 and has just recently begun to generate additional revenues.

DISCUSSION QUESTIONS

Note to students: Many of the discussion questions and exercises are open-ended, designed to stimulate your ability to analyze auditing problems. Often, as in a real audit, there is no absolutely correct answer. You must evaluate the facts and attempt to arrive at a logical conclusion or a viable course of action. To guide your analysis, you may want to consult a standard auditing textbook, the "Statements on Auditing Standards" issued by the Auditing Standards Board, or any other relevant authoritative pronouncements produced by the AICPA and the PCAOB.

(1) What are the main duties of each of the positions that comprise Abernethy and Chapman's engagement team (i.e., partner, manager, senior auditor, and staff auditor)?

(2) What is the purpose of having both a partner-in-charge and a consulting partner on each audit engagement? Should the partners be rotated periodically? Why or why not?

(3) Can an accounting firm hope to accrue any real benefit from a marketing campaign such as the one carried out by Abernethy and Chapman? Should the management of a company select its auditors based on advertisements alone?

(4) Larger (often national or international) CPA firms have acquired many smaller firms. Why might a large organization consider purchasing an accounting firm such as Abernethy and Chapman? Why might Abernethy and Chapman agree to be acquired? Are such mergers good for the auditing profession, generally speaking?

(5) The case stated that, during busy periods, individuals may move from one area of the firm to another, for example from consulting services to assurance services. Are there any potential problems with these movements within the firm?

EXERCISE

(1) Review the quality control standards of Abernethy and Chapman, and prepare a memo to Ms. Malott addressing the firm's policies. From the information provided, how does the firm appear to meet or not meet each of the quality control standards? If additional information is needed, state what information you would need to have to make the assessment. What recommendations for improvements do you have for the firm? Be sure to consider all of the elements of quality control as required by Standard of Quality Control Standards No. 7, *A Firm's System of Quality Control*, issued by the AICPA. The elements are (1) leadership responsibilities, (2) relevant ethical requirements, (3) acceptance and continuation of clients, (4) human

resources, (5) engagement performance, and (6) monitoring. [See template "IntroCase-1.doc"].

APPLY YOUR RESEARCH

Use library resources such as searchable databases to research the following topic.

(1)   Write a report discussing marketing by public accounting firms. Indicate the reasons that marketing is permitted and the type of marketing (particularly advertising) that has occurred. Discuss the success that firms have achieved and the reaction of accountants to marketing, especially advertising. What are the restrictions on advertising by a CPA?

CONSULTING PARTNER REVIEW

The Prentice Hall website (www.pearsonhighered.com/arens) includes audio clips prepared by the consulting partner on the audit team. This partner offers additional questions that require critical thinking about the subject material of the cases. You will listen to the clips, read any material related to the clips, perform additional research, and prepare additional memos or reports.

Bob Zimmerman will be serving as the consulting partner on the Lakeside Company audit engagement. In most of the subsequent cases, Mr. Zimmerman will be asking you additional questions about the audit of the Lakeside Company.

THE IMPACT OF SARBANES-OXLEY

(1)   The case states that the firm of Abernethy and Chapman is considering the acceptance of clients that are publicly traded. What specific steps would the firm have to take before they could accept an audit client that is publicly traded?

(2)   Discussion question #2 above addresses audit engagement management, consulting partners and rotation. Discuss how Sarbanes-Oxley has affected these issues.

The Lakeside Company: Auditing Cases

1. ANALYSIS OF A POTENTIAL AUDIT CLIENT

Benjamin M. Rogers is the president of the Lakeside Company, a retailer and distributor of consumer electronics (such as televisions) based in Richmond, Virginia. Although King and Company CPAs, a Richmond firm, had previously audited Lakeside, Rogers has recently become aware of the CPA firm of Abernethy and Chapman from reading several advertisements. His interest in the firm was heightened when he discovered that Abernethy and Chapman audits the primary bank with which he does business. During March of 2012, Rogers contacted his banker who arranged for Rogers to have lunch with one of the CPA firm's partners. At that time, a wide-ranging conversation was held concerning Lakeside as well as Abernethy and Chapman. Rogers discussed the history of the consumer electronics company along with his hopes for the future. The partner, in turn, described many of the attributes possessed by his public accounting firm. Subsequently, Rogers requested a formal appointment with Richard Abernethy, the managing partner of Abernethy and Chapman, in hopes of arriving at a final conclusion concerning Lakeside's 2012 audit engagement.

A June 1 meeting was held at the accounting firm's Richmond office and was attended by Abernethy, Rogers, and Wallace Andrews, an audit manager with the CPA firm who would be assisting in the investigation of this prospective client. Both auditors were quite interested in learning as much as possible about the consumer electronics business. Although a number of similar operations are located in the Richmond area, Abernethy and Chapman has never had a client in this field. Thus, the Lakeside engagement would offer an excellent opportunity to break into a new market.

During a rather lengthy conversation with Rogers, Abernethy and Andrews were able to obtain a significant quantity of data about the Lakeside Company and the possible audit engagement. Included in this information were the following facts:

- Rogers originally began Lakeside in 1993 as a single store that sold bargain-priced televisions and stereo equipment. This business did well and the company expanded thereafter at the rate of one new store every two or three years. Presently six stores are in operation, three in Richmond with one in each of three nearby cities: Charlottesville, Fredericksburg, and Petersburg. The first five were set up in rented space within small shopping centers. However, the most recent store was located in a building constructed by Lakeside itself, adjacent to a new shopping mall on the east side of Richmond. In addition, Lakeside owns a warehouse that also provides office space for the company's administrative staff. The growth to date has been slow and has not produced the benefits and profitability that Rogers has expected. He is looking for a way to increase the growth rate and taking the company public is beginning to look like the only way that sufficient resources can be amassed.

- In 2005, Lakeside reduced the marketing of bargain-priced electronics in a move to concentrate on the sale of high-end audio and video equipment. Several years later, Lakeside became the sole distributor of Cypress Products for the states of Virginia and North Carolina. Cypress is the manufacturer of a quality line of audio and video equipment. Shortly thereafter, the Lakeside stores began to carry Cypress products almost exclusively. Despite the quality of Cypress equipment, the brand was not well known in the Richmond area and store revenues ("retail sales") began to decline. Sales did rebound somewhat in 2010 and 2011, although Rogers admitted to Abernethy that all of the stores had suffered from intense competition and a poor economy within the local market. He even indicated that a small audio equipment company, consisting of two stores, had gone bankrupt in Richmond during the past six months. However, he was not certain as to the specific cause of that failure. He believes that a larger organization could take advantage of combined management, purchasing, and storage. Geographically there are several cities that Lakeside could enter without dramatically increasing the distances from its current warehouse.

- To market the Cypress brand across the states of Virginia and North Carolina, Lakeside had hired a staff of six sales representatives who visit audio, electronics, and appliance stores in their geographic region. These other retailers could then order merchandise from Lakeside by telephoning the Richmond headquarters/warehouse. After a credit check, requested inventory is shipped to these customers and billed at 2/10; n/45. Up to 20% of the merchandise can be returned to Lakeside within four months as long as the goods have not been damaged. In the past, returns have been low. Rogers indicated that these "distributorship sales" had initially been disappointing but had risen materially in the last two years as the Cypress reputation began to spread. Rogers has only begun to consider what a more comprehensive Southeast strategy would require in terms of sales administration and logistics.

- Audio and video equipment inventory is purchased weekly from Cypress. Regional distributors such as Lakeside are allowed 90-day terms, but Cypress encourages quick payment by offering large cash discounts. In hopes of maintaining a high profit margin, Rogers has chosen to take all available discounts. To meet the payment terms, Lakeside holds bank credit lines with two Richmond banks totaling $1,500,000. Interest on this debt is based on the floating prime rate of the respective banks and has averaged around 5% to 8% during recent years. Both banks require that cash in an amount equal to 5% of the outstanding credit line remain on deposit.

- The company's warehouse and the sixth store were constructed with funds provided by loans from the National Insurance Company of Virginia. The first of these obligations was obtained at a 6.5% annual interest rate while the second holds a rate of 8%.

- Rogers stated that he was quite unhappy with the services of his present CPA firm, King and Company. He enumerated three grievances that he had with that organization. First, he felt the firm had provided little assistance in updating Lakeside's accounting systems. Lakeside was simply outgrowing the control features of its current systems, and Rogers asserted that King and Company had not provided the needed input for upgrading them. Second, Rogers believed that King and Company was charging an excessive fee for its annual audit. He stated that he was no longer willing to pay that much money for what he termed were inferior services.

- Rogers' final problem with King and Company revolved around the audit opinion that was rendered on Lakeside's financial statements for the year ending December 31, 2011. The auditors issued a qualified opinion. King and Company believed that the value of Lakeside's $186,000 investment in its latest store had been impaired based on guidelines established by the FASB. However, Rogers disagreed and refused to write down the reported value of the property. The sixth store, which opened in November of 2010, was constructed adjacent to a shopping center that had proven to be very unsuccessful. To date, the shopping center has leased less than 40 percent of its available space. The Lakeside store has, consequently, never been able to generate the customer traffic necessary to even come close to its break-even point. The continuing failures of the shopping center made the fate of the Lakeside store appear quite uncertain to King and Company. Furthermore, the CPA firm felt that Lakeside would have considerable trouble in disposing of the store if that became necessary. Because Rogers continued to report this asset based on historical cost, the firm felt that a material misstatement existed and issued a qualified opinion. Rogers expressed annoyance with a firm that would stifle his growth plans and wondered what it would be like if his expansion plans were to become a reality.

- Lakeside Company is owned by a group of eight investors. Rogers (who is 46 years old) owns 30% of the outstanding stock while the remaining seven stockholders individually possess between 6% and 22% of the company's shares. Although all of the investors live in the Richmond area, only Rogers is involved actively in the day-to-day operations of the business. The Board of Directors is comprised of Rogers, two other owners, and two other local residents who are not owners. Three board members, including the two non-owners, comprise the audit committee. When the company was first organized, all eight shareholders agreed that an audit by an independent CPA firm would be held annually. This same requirement was also a stipulation made by the banks participating in Lakeside's financing.

- A manager and an assistant manager operate each of the six stores. Normally, three to six sales clerks also work at each outlet on a part-time basis. In hopes of stimulating lagging store sales, Rogers initiated a bonus system during 2011, which already appears to be boosting revenues. Under this plan, every manager and assistant manager will receive a cash bonus each January based on the income earned by his or her store during the previous year. The bonus figure is a percentage of the gross profit of the store less any directly allocable expenses.

- Lakeside Company is in the process of opening a new (seventh) store, which will begin operations by December of 2012. Earlier this year Rogers formed his own separate corporation to construct this latest facility. Upon completion, the building will be leased to Lakeside for its entire life. Although Rogers was confident that this new store would do well, he wanted to avoid any further accounting problems associated with the uncertainty of success. He is also investigating land purchases in at least four other locations in the Southeast.

- Rogers indicated to Abernethy that growth was one of his primary business objectives. He stated that the Cypress distributorship offered unlimited opportunity and that, once firmly established, each of the Lakeside stores was a sound financial investment.

- To finance its growth, the company is considering a public offering of stock.

- The company is strongly contemplating the addition of computer equipment to its product line.

DISCUSSION QUESTIONS

(1) Why would the owners of Lakeside as well as the company's banks require that an independent CPA firm perform an annual audit?

(2) This case implies that no auditor with the firm of Abernethy and Chapman has an in-depth understanding of the consumer electronics industry. Is a CPA firm allowed to accept an engagement without having established the necessary expertise to oversee the audit? Would the knowledge required to audit a consumer electronics company differ significantly from that needed in the examination of a car dealership? Does the auditor have an obligation to discuss his lack of expertise, or his plans to obtain the expertise with the client?

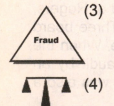

(3) Auditors must assess the possibility of fraud risk factors. Fraud risk factors are events or situations that would indicate an increased possibility that fraud has occurred. Lakeside has recently created a profit-sharing bonus plan. Why might such an incentive be a special concern to an auditor?

(4) Rogers wants Abernethy and Chapman to assist his company in developing new accounting systems. Does a CPA firm face an independence problem in auditing the output of systems that the same firm designed and installed? Does your answer depend on if the client is publicly traded or not? How so?

4

(5) After the discussion at the CPA firm, Andrews was assigned to visit the headquarters/warehouse of Lakeside to tour the facility. What should Andrews observe, and what factors should he be especially aware of during this visit?

(6) Is there any reason why Lakeside might not want to hire a CPA firm that has other clients in the electronics industry?

EXERCISES

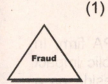

(1) According to Statement on Auditing Standards, *Consideration of Fraud in a Financial Statement Audit*, the auditor should consider whether the information indicates that one or more fraud risk factors are present. Fraud risk factors are potential problems or indicators of potential fraud. Three conditions that are typically present when fraud exists: an *incentive or pressure* to perpetrate fraud, an *opportunity* to carry out the fraud, and the *attitude* to justify the fraudulent action. Based on the conference with Rogers, perform the following [Case1-1.doc]:

a) List the fraud risk factors that the CPA firm might encounter if they accept this audit engagement. Be sure to include a discussion of all items that will probably require special attention during the audit. You should find at least 10 fraud risk factors.

b) For each of these fraud risk factors, indicate how the auditor should follow up on each potential problem if the engagement is accepted. Consider how Abernethy and Chapman should include the fraud assessment in conducting the audit.

(2) Based upon discussion in the case, prepare the auditor's report that King and Company rendered at the end of the year 2011 engagement. How does this opinion differ from a standard auditor's report? [Case1-2.doc]

APPLY YOUR RESEARCH

Use library resources such as searchable databases to research the following topic.

(1) The periodic selection of a new auditing firm by a company is not an uncommon practice. Write a report discussing auditor changes. Why do companies change auditors? What kinds of disclosures are required when a company changes auditors? Are companies allowed to merely "shop around" for the audit opinion they desire? Does this seem ethical to you?

CONSULTING PARTNER REVIEW

Bob Zimmerman, the consulting partner on the Lakeside engagement, is concerned about the following issues and would like for you to respond to them. The audio clips are available online at www.prenhall.com/arens.

(1) The reliance of Lakeside on Cypress products.

(2)   The impact of poor client operating systems on an audit engagement.

(3)   Testing for long-lived asset impairment.

THE IMPACT OF SARBANES-OXLEY

(1)   According to this case, the Lakeside Company is considering a public offering of stock to finance its growth. What steps would the Lakeside Company have to take before issuing stock to the public? In particular, how would the provisions of the Sarbanes-Oxley Act impact this decision? How does the possible public sale of stocks impact the Lakeside Company financial reporting requirements?

(2)   Explain how the acceptance of a public company would impact a CPA firm. In particular, how would Roger's decision about offering stock to the public impact Abernethy and Chapman's decision of whether or not to accept Lakeside as a client?

6

The Lakeside Company: Auditing Cases

2. NEW CLIENTS, LEGAL LIABILITY AND MATERIALITY

During August of 2010, the Virginia-based CPA firm of Abernethy and Chapman underwent a peer review of its quality control procedures and its quality control document. Although the final report of the outside review team was favorable, it did criticize the lack of control demonstrated in accepting new audit engagements. Until that time, this decision was left solely to the managing partner who often made little or no investigation of a potential client before committing the firm's services. The review team pointed out that this policy failed to protect the firm against becoming involved in engagements with undesirable clients.

Following the peer review, Abernethy and Chapman created a three-partner committee to screen each potential client. This group, called the Client Screening Committee, was empowered to make the ultimate decision as to whether the firm should actively seek a particular audit. Under guidelines established by this committee, a partner was put in charge of researching any possible new engagement. This partner had to complete several forms and provide other data describing every potential client. The partner also had to attach a final recommendation letter evaluating the wisdom of seeking the audit. The committee would then review all of this documentation and instruct the partner as to the appropriate course of action.

The addition of a client with potential plans to go public in the next few years will bring Abernethy and Chapman under the regulations of the PCAOB. In order to adequately plan this increased regulation and impact on the firm's practice, Richard Abernethy also asked Bob Zimmerman to evaluate how their client review process would interact with the registration process. The partners are now considering whether they wish to become registered and are actively assessing the resources they would need to commit to such a strategy.

Regardless of the decision to become registered, Abernethy and Chapman's client review process requires the following two documents to be completed for each new engagement—"Analysis of Potential Legal Liability" and "Information from Predecessor Auditor" (presented in Exhibits 2-1 and 2-2). Before completing these forms, the in-charge partner learns as much as possible about the potential client and its industry. For example, either the partner or a member of the audit staff reviews recent annual reports and tax returns, tours the company facilities, reads any applicable AICPA Industry Audit Guides, and talks with the business references furnished by the potential client. In addition, the partner always discusses the new engagement with the company's predecessor auditors. To keep from burdening the predecessor auditor with inquiries from numerous firms, the discussion is only made after the engagement has been offered to a specific new firm.

In investigating the Lakeside Company, Richard Abernethy was aware that much might be learned from a conference with the predecessor CPA firm, King and Company. Once the Lakeside engagement had been offered to Abernethy and Chapman, the partner began to seek a meeting with the predecessor auditor. Because of the confidential nature of audit information, arrangements for this discussion were made through Benjamin Rogers, president of Lakeside. An appointment was scheduled for June 15, 2012 so that Abernethy could talk with William King, the managing partner of King and Company.

At this meeting, King did not appear to be surprised that the Lakeside Company was seeking a new independent auditing firm. He talked quite candidly with Abernethy about the engagement. "I assumed when we qualified our year 2011 opinion that it would be our last year on the job. Rogers is really interested in stimulating growth and becoming president of a large company. He never talked about going public with me, but I am not surprised. I am positive that he did not like taking that 'impairment of value' problem to his stockholders or to the banks that finance his inventory. That could scare them and put a damper on his expansion.

"I was comfortable working with Rogers. He and all of the members of his organization appear to be people of integrity. However, he was always unhappy with our fees. Have you discussed with him how much the audit will cost if he goes forward with his public offering? I honestly don't believe that he understands the purpose of an audit or all of the work that the job entails.

"I must admit that Rogers argued vehemently against writing down the reported value of the sixth store. He based his arguments on two points: first, that no real impairment existed, and second, that even if Store 6 represented an impairment, the potential loss was not material. As to the impairment issue, our firm was never able to satisfy itself that Lakeside was not going to be stuck holding a totally worthless building in a failed shopping center. Rogers simply disagreed; he could only see the most optimistic possibilities for that store. Unfortunately, the materiality question was even more complex. The company has a net investment of approximately $186,000 in that store out of $3.6 million in total assets. Rogers contended that, at the very worse, he could sell the building for around $100,000. Of course, that's all in his crystal ball. We obtained an appraisal that came in at $150,000. With the company having a net worth of less than a million dollars, our partners felt that write-off of the potential asset impairment was absolutely necessary. When he would not recognize this loss, we felt that a material misstatement existed within the financial statements and a qualification was required.

"The company's situation is really quite unique. The audio and video equipment retail stores are only marginal operations. Rogers ruined them when he turned them into Cypress outlets. The market in the Richmond area is just not strong enough for that particular brand alone. On the other hand, he has done exceptionally well with the distributorship side of the business. Across Virginia and North Carolina a very large potential demand seems to have developed for Cypress products. I can see why he is planning on major growth in his distributorship business. Rogers is just now beginning to tap into that market. Consequently, he is trying to operate one stagnant and one prospering business at the same time. I certainly foresee the distributorship sales growing rapidly over the next few years. I will be interested in seeing how well the internal systems of the company are able to adapt to that expansion, especially since Rogers dislikes spending any money. Does he know what it will cost to meet PCAOB standards in the area of his internal control?'"

Before ending the conversation, King assured Abernethy that their audit documentation of past examinations would be available for review if Abernethy and Chapman were retained to do Lakeside's current audit. The audit documentation of King and Company consisted of a permanent file of information gathered about Lakeside and annual files containing all of the evidence accumulated during each of the previous yearly examinations.

If the firm decides to accept this engagement, then the engagement team must establish a preliminary judgment about materiality. This judgment normally takes place during the planning phase of the audit. However, due to significant uncertainty surrounding Store 6, the Client Screening Committee asked Wallace Andrews, a manager in the firm, to complete the form "A Preliminary Judgment about Materiality" (presented in Exhibit 2-3) to see just how material a potential write-down of Store 6 would be.

Andrews must decide on the combined amount of misstatement in the financial statements that the firm would consider material. *Materiality* is the amount of a misstatement on the financial statements that makes it probable that a reasonable user of the financial statements would change his or her decision due to this misstatement. For example, if the net income of Lakeside was overstated by one million dollars, would that change the decision of a creditor to loan money to the company? What if net income was only overstated by $100?

Andrews will consider both quantitative and qualitative factors in determining the preliminary judgment about materiality. He knows that materiality is a relative rather than an absolute concept, meaning that the size of the client impacts the level of materiality. Because materiality is relative, it is necessary to have quantitative bases for establishing whether misstatements are material. A base is a critical item of which financial statement users tend to focus while making decisions. The base will vary depending on the nature of the client's business. Typical bases include net income before taxes, net sales, total assets, and stockholders' equity. For example, Wallace might determine that 3% to 5% of net income before taxes is a reasonable range for the quantitative part of the preliminary judgment. Wallace will also consider qualitative factors. Certain types of misstatements are likely to be more important to users than others, even if the dollar amounts are the same. For example, misstatements that involve fraud may be more important to users than misstatements due to unintentional errors. Fraud reflects on the integrity of management and other employees of the client. For example, if the firm suspects fraud, Wallace might choose the lower end of the range determined in quantitative part as the preliminary judgment about materiality.

DISCUSSION QUESTIONS

(1) King and Company faced a materiality question in forming its year 2011 audit opinion. How do auditors evaluate the materiality of an item in a specific engagement? Do you believe that the possible impairment of the investment in the sixth store was actually material to the Lakeside Company?

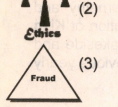

(2) If Rogers had not consented in having Abernethy talk with the predecessor auditor, what actions would have been open to Abernethy?

(3) If Abernethy had learned from King that Rogers or his staff lacked integrity, what action should have then been followed and why?

(4) What is the purpose of a peer review? Why have peer reviews become necessary? What does the peer review team examine?

(5) What is the purpose of audit documentation, and what general data should be found in (a) a permanent file and (b) a current analysis file?

(6) King mentioned that Rogers did not fully comprehend the purpose of an audit. What obligation does a CPA firm have to ensure that a client understands the audit function? What additional auditing procedures will need to be performed if Lakeside does go public?

(7) Rogers apparently does not like paying for an audit. Should Abernethy suggest that a review rather than an audit be made of Lakeside's financial statements? What is the difference between a review and an audit? What would be the financial impact of an audit on the level of fees if Lakeside were to go public?

(8) Richard Abernethy has to make a recommendation to the partner review committee as to whether the CPA firm should seek the audit engagement of the Lakeside Company. If you were Abernethy, what would you recommend?

EXERCISES

(1) Review Exhibits 2-1 and 2-2. From the information that has been presented in the first two cases, complete these two forms [Case2-1.doc].

(2)   If the firm of Abernethy and Chapman does accept this audit engagement, an assessment will be made of the audit documentation produced by the predecessor auditor. Prepare a list of the specific contents of the King and Company audit documentation that should be evaluated by Abernethy and Chapman. Indicate each area that should be addressed and the purpose of studying these particular areas of the audit documentation. For example, one item that Abernethy and Chapman should review is the adjusting entries proposed by King and Company resulting from their audit. Abernethy and Chapman should examine these to determine the type and materiality of the proposed adjustments. [Case2-2.doc]

(3)   Determine the preliminary judgment about materiality for the Lakeside audit as a whole. Express your answer as a dollar amount. Determine the appropriate level of materiality based on an analysis of the information in this case and Case 1. Also, use the financial statement information presented in Case 3 for the quantitative portion (see Exhibits 3-4, 3-5 and 3-6). Fully support and discuss the materiality level that you determine. Document your analysis by completing the form in Exhibit 2-3. Based on this materiality level, would the impairment loss be material if the carrying value of Store 6 is completely impaired? What if half the carrying value is impaired? How might this impact the firm's decision whether or not to accept the Lakeside engagement? [Case2-3.doc]

(4)   Assume that Abernethy and Chapman audits Lakeside's 2012 financial statements and gathers sufficient, competent evidence to render an unqualified opinion without any mention of the impairment. Assume further that Lakeside opts to issue comparative statements showing figures for 2011 and 2012. Write a single audit report that will inform the reader of both opinions as well as the examination made by the previous auditors. [Case2-4.doc]

APPLY YOUR RESEARCH

Use library resources such as searchable databases to research the following topics.

(1)   Write a report describing the purpose of a peer review. Discuss the reasons that peer reviews have become necessary and the type of examination that is performed.

(2)   King and Company had to make a decision as to the materiality of a potential problem. Write a report describing the methods used by auditors in making this type of judgment.

(3)   The auditor's exposure to lawsuits has been increasing over the last few decades. Write a report describing the profession's exposure to legal liability. Why has the auditor's exposure to liability been increasing? What has the profession done to deal with this situation?

11

CONSULTING PARTNER REVIEW

Bob Zimmerman, the consulting partner on the Lakeside engagement, is concerned about the following issues and would like for you to respond to them. The audio clips are available online at www.pearsonhighered.com/arens.

(1)   Estimating future cash flows and current market value.
(2)   Preliminary assessment of materiality.

THE IMPACT OF SARBANES-OXLEY

(1)   According to Case 1, the Lakeside Company is considering a public offering of stock to finance its growth. The firm of Abernethy and Chapman does not presently have any audit clients that are public companies. What steps would Abernethy and Chapman have to take before accepting a public company as a client? In particular, how would the Sarbanes-Oxley Act impact the firm's decision to accept such a company as an audit client? What additional requirements are there for a CPA firm that is registered to practice before the SEC compared with a CPA firm that is not registered? Is the firm of Abernethy and Chapman capable of meeting these standards?

(2)   According to Case 1, the Lakeside Company is considering a public offering of stock to finance its growth. What additional requirements are there for a publicly traded company compared with a nonpublic company? What issues have arisen so far in the case that should be addressed as Lakeside considers going public?

Exhibit 2-1

Abernethy and Chapman

ANALYSIS OF POTENTIAL LEGAL LIABILITY

Potential Client:

Type of Engagement:

Form Completed By: _____ Date:_____

(1) Is the potential client privately held or publicly held?

(2) Evaluate the possible liability to the client that Abernethy and Chapman might incur, if the engagement is accepted.

(3) List the third parties that presently have a financial association with the potential client and could be expected to see the financial statements. These parties are also called primary and foreseen beneficiaries.

(4) Discuss the possibility that other third parties will be brought into a position where they would be expected to see the financial statements of the potential client. These parties are also called foreseeable beneficiaries.

(5) Evaluate the possible legal liability to third parties, both present and potential, that Abernethy and Chapman might incur if the engagement is accepted.

Exhibit 2-2

Abernethy and Chapman

INFORMATION FROM PREDECESSOR AUDITOR

Potential Client:

Form Completed By:

Predecessor Auditor:

Date of Interview:

(1)   Discuss the predecessor auditor's evaluation of the integrity of the management of the potential client.

(2)   Did the predecessor auditor reveal any disagreements with management as to accounting principles, auditing procedures, or other similarly significant matters? If so, fully describe these disagreements.

(3)   What was the predecessor auditor's understanding as to the reasons for the change in auditors?

(4)   Did the predecessor auditor give any indication of other significant audit problems associated with the potential client?

(5)   Did the predecessor auditor indicate any problem in allowing Abernethy and Chapman to review prior years' audit documentation for the potential client? If "yes," explain.

(6)   Was the predecessor auditor's response limited in any way?

14

Exhibit 2-3

Abernethy and Chapman
Preliminary Judgment about Materiality

Client: _____

Balance Sheet Date: _____

Prepared by: _____

Determine the preliminary judgment about materiality for the client as a whole. Express your answer as a dollar amount. Determine the appropriate level of materiality based on all analyses completed for the client thus far. Fully support and discuss the materiality level that you determine.

Quantitative Considerations: Because materiality is relative, it is necessary to have bases for establishing whether misstatements are material. A base is a critical item of which users tend to focus while making decisions. The base will vary depending on the nature of the client's business. Typical bases may include net income before taxes, net sales, total assets and stockholders' equity. Percentages typically range from 1% to 10% depending on the base.

Base (from previous year)	Dollar Amount of Base	Percentage Range	Base x Percentage

Qualitative Considerations: Certain types of misstatements are likely to be more important to users than others, even if the dollar amounts are the same. For example, misstatements that involve fraud may be more important to users than misstatements due to unintentional errors. Fraud reflects on the integrity of management and other employees of the client.

Item to be Considered	Impact on Materiality (Increase or Decrease)

Preliminary Judgment about Materiality: Combine the quantitative and qualitative considerations into one overall materiality level.

Materiality level:	$

Discussion: Discuss how you arrived at this dollar amount for the preliminary judgment about materiality. That is, how did you combine the qualitative and quantitative considerations to arrive at this dollar amount?

15

The Lakeside Company:
Auditing Cases

3. AUDIT RISK AND ANALYTICAL PROCEDURES

On June 28, 2012, Richard Abernethy, managing partner of Abernethy and Chapman, met with the firm's three-member engagement review committee to discuss the Lakeside Company audit. He believes that issue of Lakeside's public offering can be considered as a separate issue from the client acceptance. Although Abernethy admits that the job has some problems, he strongly recommends seeking Lakeside as an audit client. He describes Lakeside as an established Richmond company with an almost unlimited growth potential through the distributorship side of its business. Furthermore, he believes that the engagement offers an excellent opportunity for Abernethy and Chapman to gain entry into a new audit area: consumer electronics. If the public offering goes forward, Abernethy and Chapman can choose to be registered, or can arrange for an orderly transfer to another CPA firm at that time.

Abernethy indicated that he had talked with King and Company, the predecessor auditors. Abernethy not only described the controversy that had arisen over the auditor's 2011 qualified opinion but also said that King and Company appeared to have no reservations about the integrity of Lakeside's management. In addition, if retained, Abernethy and Chapman would be allowed to review the prior years' audit documentation. Wallace Andrews, an audit manager with Abernethy and Chapman, then described to the committee his visit to the Lakeside Company headquarters. He found many elements of the company's accounting system to be more appropriate to a smaller business but still judged that the financial records were capable of being audited.

After reviewing all of the pertinent information, the review committee unanimously recommended that the firm accept this engagement. Consequently, Abernethy met with Benjamin Rogers, president of Lakeside, during the subsequent week and a final oral agreement was reached. At this meeting, Abernethy presented Rogers with a report that highlights the impact of the public offering on Lakeside, on the audit fees, on Abernethy and Chapman, and on the accounting and control issues that would likely develop. Rogers was not put off by the potential problems, and seemed to appreciate that Abernethy was trying to help him make this difficult decision. Rogers has agreed to consider this additional information and consult with Abernethy as he makes the final decision to go public. He will be seeking alternative financing in the short-term so that his expansion plans can continue.

Several days later, Abernethy forwarded two copies of an engagement letter (see Exhibit 3-1) to Rogers, who signed one copy and returned it to the CPA firm. Rogers also contacted the previous auditors, King and Company, and gave them formal permission to show the Lakeside audit documentation to Abernethy and Chapman.

Three members of the organization were assigned to the engagement team and began to plan the audit. The members of the team included Dan Cline, partner; Wallace Andrews, manager; and Carole Mitchell, senior auditor. In addition, several staff auditors were available to assist this group whenever necessary. There was also a consulting partner, Bob Zimmerman, assigned. Although each of these auditors was involved in completing other engagements, a number of preliminary audit procedures were started during the months that followed. As the partner, Cline was responsible for the final review of all audit documentation produced during the Lakeside examination. To acquire the industry expertise needed to evaluate the client's financial reporting, he set out to learn as much as possible about the selling and distribution of consumer electronics.

Dan Cline convened an audit planning session to discuss audit risk and the materiality level. All potential members of the team were present and participated in the brain-storming session. The team reviewed the fraud risk factors or potential problem areas that were previously determined by the firm (see Case 1). An independent auditor provides reasonable, not absolute, assurance; therefore, risk is not entirely eliminated. For the Lakeside engagement overall, and for each separate account or group of accounts, Abernethy and Chapman confronts an amount of risk called *acceptable audit risk*.

Acceptable audit risk (AAR) is a measure of how willing the auditor is to accept that the financial statements may be materially misstated even after the audit is completed and an unqualified ("clean") opinion is given. If the firm desires a low level of risk, then they have to be more certain that the financial statements are not materially misstated. For example, if the AAR is 10%, then the auditor has to be 90% confident that the financial statements are fairly stated, and if the AAR is 5%, then the auditor has to be 95% confident. Thus, there is an inverse relationship between the AAR and the firm's confidence in the fair presentation of the financial statements.

There are three components to AAR: inherent risk, control risk, and planned detection risk. *Inherent risk* (IR) is a measure of the susceptibility of material misstatement before considering the effectiveness of the internal control. The evaluation of inherent risk is based upon the nature of the client's business and the susceptibility to misstatement in particular accounts. For example, due to the possibility of theft and the large number of transactions affecting the account, "cash" is normally considered to have a higher level of inherent risk than "prepaid expenses." The auditor does not affect inherent risk, rather he or she seeks to assess the level within the client. Auditors evaluate these risks for the engagement as a whole and for each account and/or accounting cycle. The risks are typically stated either in qualitative terms such as *high*, *moderate,* or *low risk*, or in quantitative terms.

Control risk is a measure of the firm's assessment of the likelihood that a material misstatement will not be prevented or detected by the client's internal control. The evaluation of control risk is based upon the effectiveness of Lakeside's internal control. For example, if the engagement team concludes that Lakeside's internal control is poor, then control risk will be set at the maximum level. Like inherent risk, the auditor does not affect control risk, rather, he or she seeks to assess the level within the client.

Planned detection risk is a measure of the firm's assessment of the likelihood that material misstatements that go undetected by the client's internal control will also go undetected by the firm's own audit procedures. The acceptable level of planned detection risk for an audit is inversely related to the firm's assessment of inherent risk and control risk. If the inherent risk and the control risk are judged to be high for a particular account or the company as a whole, then the acceptable level of planned detection risk is low. With planned detection risk at a low level, the auditor must plan to do more (or a higher quality of) substantive testing.

In the planning stage of the audit, Andrews began to assess inherent risk by gaining an in-depth knowledge of Lakeside. He reviewed the audit documentation of the predecessor auditor and spent a number of days at Lakeside's headquarters studying various aspects of the business while also talking with key employees. In addition, he toured three of the retail stores and, at another time, questioned two of the regional sales representatives about the organization of the company's distributorship business.

Mitchell, the senior auditor, is in charge of making a preliminary assessment of control risk. In the initial stages of the engagement, she and staff auditor Art Heyman are evaluating the five components of internal control (see Case 4 for this evaluation).

Based on the assessments of inherent and control risks, Mitchell will determine the acceptable level of planned detection risk, which will allow her to recommend substantive auditing procedures for the Lakeside engagement. These substantive procedures will be capable (according to her judgment) of generating the sufficient, competent evidence needed to render a decision as to the fair presentation of the financial statements. However, before Mitchell's program is put into action, a review by both Cline and Andrews will be required. In most audits, the partner and manager are likely to feel that additional testing is needed in certain audit areas whereas less evidence may be adequate in others.

The partners of Abernethy and Chapman stress that risk levels must be constantly monitored throughout an engagement. Hence, before the final audit program is prepared, a thorough investigation is made to identify all critical audit areas within the client's financial records. *A critical area* is defined by the firm as any account balance, any procedure within a system, or any potential problem where either the materiality or the risk of material misstatement is so great as to threaten the fairness of the reported data. Although Mitchell understands that the determination of critical areas will influence the specific testing procedures to be included within the audit program, she also realizes that her firm has submitted a relatively low bid to get this engagement. Thus, she is aware that wasted time has to be avoided in order to complete the examination within the budgeted time period. By pinpointing any critical areas, Mitchell hopes to maximize audit efficiency.

One of the principal techniques used during the assessment of inherent risk and to identify critical audit areas is called *analytical procedures*. Analytical procedures are considered so important that they are required to be performed during the initial planning stage and again at the final stage of the audit. According to auditing standards (AU 329), the objective of analytical procedures "is to identify such things as the existence of unusual transactions and events, and amounts, ratios and trends that might indicate matters that have financial statement and audit planning ramifications." Analytical procedures do not necessarily indicate that a balance is correctly or incorrectly reported. However, if a recorded amount differs significantly from the expectation, additional investigation is warranted. There are five types of analytical procedures--those that compare the client's data with:

1) industry data (such as industry average financial ratios),
2) similar prior-period data (such as account balances in the previous year),
3) client-determined expected results (such as budgeted amounts),
4) expected results using non-financial information (such as square footage and shelf space in a warehouse to estimate maximum inventory quantities), and
5) auditor-determined expected results (such as estimates from historical trends in accounts or financial ratios).

One of the most commonly applied analytical review procedures is called *financial ratio analysis*. Using this method allows an auditor to identify relationships among accounts that help to measure a company's liquidity, solvency, and profitability. A summary of some typical financial ratios is included in Exhibit 3-2. An auditor can use these ratios to identify trends from prior periods or to compare with other companies in the same industry. Exhibit 3-3 includes average ratios of companies in Lakeside's industry: consumer electronics.

Mitchell visited the Lakeside headquarters on October 17, 2012, to begin performing analytical procedures on that company's financial information for the first nine months of the current year. Prior to this date, she had carefully reviewed the Lakeside financial statements for the past two years (Exhibits 3-4, 3-5, and 3-6). She also studied industry data developed for her by the audit partner, Dan Cline (Exhibit 3-3).

When Mitchell arrived at the client's headquarters, she obtained from the controller's office a trial balance for the first nine months of the current and previous years (Exhibit 3-7). Before beginning her analysis, she discussed the general ledger and trial balance procedures with Mark Hayes, the controller for Lakeside. He indicated that a trial balance is prepared every two weeks to provide company officials with current data. Copies of this trial balance are distributed to Mr. Rogers, Mr. Miller, Ms. Howell, Mr. Davis, and Mr. Thomas for their review (see Exhibit 4-1 for an organization chart). All ledger entries, except for inventory and cost of goods sold, come from a weekly posting of the company's journals. The various inventory figures are generated from a weekly summary sheet provided by the computer center that maintains Lakeside's perpetual inventory records. At the end of each quarter, estimated figures for depreciation and bonuses are included to present a more realistic net income figure for the period. Income taxes are also estimated by Hayes and paid quarterly to the government. In addition, to promote comparability in evaluating the stores, a monthly rental charge is included for Store 6. This figure, which is based on square footage and store location, is eliminated prior to preparation of external financial statements. However, company management believes that this expense is necessary for internal comparisons and decision making.

DISCUSSION QUESTIONS

(1)   An independent auditor must document that an understanding of the audit engagement has been established with the client. An engagement letter is one method that can be used for this documentation. Why is this documentation required, and what should be included? Analyze the engagement letter prepared by Abernethy and Chapman (Exhibit 3-1). What specific responsibilities is the CPA firm accepting? What responsibilities are assigned to the client company?

(2)   A client company will report balances for accounts such as Cost of Goods Sold. In order to perform analytical procedures, the auditor must develop expectations from as many sources as possible. The expected balance is then compared with the actual balance and any significant fluctuations are examined further. In the Lakeside case, what sources would be available to the auditor in arriving at an expected figure for Cost of Goods Sold?

(3)   What potential problem areas would be inherent in auditing a business such as the Lakeside Company? In other words, what accounts or transactions would typically have a high level of inherent risk?

(4)   An audit program is designed to generate sufficient evidence on which the auditor can base an opinion. How does the auditor know when sufficient evidence has been accumulated?

(5)   Mitchell is going to perform analytical procedures on Lakeside's trial balance and other accounting data. What is the quality of the evidence that is gathered by this substantive testing procedure? That is, how competent is evidence provided by analytical procedures compared with other types of evidence?

(6)   How extensive should an auditor's knowledge of a client's industry be, and how does the auditor go about getting this type of information?

(7)   This case suggests that price competition with other CPA firms was an important factor in securing this audit engagement. What are the potential problems for a CPA firm that can arise from acquiring clients through price competition?

(8)   What is the relationship between control risk and planned detection risk? Also, discuss the relationship between the level of detection risk and the relative amount

20

of substantive tests (e.g., high, moderate, low) to be performed by the auditors. For example, if the detection risk is high, does that mean the auditor should perform more or less substantive tests than otherwise?

(9) How does a CPA firm assess the risk of fraud? How is this assessment related to other elements of audit risk assessment?

(10) Is it reasonable for Abernethy and Chapman to consider accepting Lakeside as a client when the firm is not currently registered with the PCAOB?

EXERCISE

(1) Using the information presented in Exhibits 3-2 through 3-7, perform the following analytical procedures. See templates [Case3-1.doc] and [Case3.xls]

(a) Compute the financial ratios listed in Exhibit 3-2 for Lakeside for the years ending December 31, 2010 and December 31, 2011. Comment on any large fluctuations, unusual fluctuations, or lack of expected fluctuations. Also, give an *overall* conclusion as to the significance of the change in Lakeside's liquidity, solvency, and profitability positions from 2010 to 2011. Use the following format for your answer.

Ratio	2010	2011	Significance of Change
Current	1.36	1.36	No significant fluctuation, indicating a stable liquidity position (based on this measure of liquidity)

(b) Compare the year 2011 financial ratios computed for Lakeside above to the industry average ratios included in Exhibit 3-3. Comment on any large fluctuations, unusual fluctuations, or lack of expected fluctuations. Also, give an *overall* conclusion as to the significance of the difference between Lakeside's liquidity, solvency, and profitability positions in 2011 and the industry average positions. Use the following format for your answers.

Ratio	Industry Ave.	Lakeside 2011	Significance of Change
Current	2.16	1.36	Lakeside is below the industry average. This may indicate short-term solvency problems

(c) Scan each of the financial statements and the trial balances included in Exhibits 3-4 through 3-7. Comment on any unusual accounts; account balances; or large, unusual, or lack of expected fluctuations from the previous year. You should find at least 10 items. Organize your answer as follows:

Procedure	Findings	Significance
Scan the trial balances.	A debit balance appears in the "Allowance for Doubtful Accounts" account. [Note: you may have more than one "finding" for each procedure].	Bad accounts may be increasing or a debit entry may have been misposted.

(2) Determine the appropriate level of inherent risk for the Lakeside Engagement as a whole, using qualitative terms (high, moderate, or low inherent risk). Based upon an analysis of the information in this case, Case 1, and Case 2, is the inherent risk for the Lakeside Company as a whole high, moderate or low? Fully support and discuss your analysis of inherent risk. Document your analysis of inherent risk by completing the form in Exhibit 3-8. The first line is completed for you as an example.

APPLY YOUR RESEARCH

Use library resources such as searchable databases to research the following topics.

(1) The assessment of risk is an important topic in auditing. Write a report identifying the types of risk that are found in an audit. Describe each of these risks. Discuss the methods by which the various risk levels are assessed by the auditor. Finally, describe the interrelationships among these risks.

(2) Write a report discussing the auditor's use of analytical procedures in conducting an audit. What are the primary analytical procedures that auditors use? Why are analytical procedures necessary on an audit? How do they help an auditor be more efficient and effective? At what stages of an audit are analytical procedures applied?

(3) Two of the biggest public companies in Lakeside's industry (consumer electronics) are Best Buy and Radio Shack. Obtain the most recent financial statements for these companies from www.sec.gov/edgar.shtml or from the companies' websites. Compute the ratios in Exhibit 3-2 for each of these companies. How does Lakeside compare with these companies in terms of liquidity, profitability, and solvency?

CONSULTING PARTNER REVIEW

Bob Zimmerman, the consulting partner on the Lakeside engagement, is concerned about the following issues and would like for you to respond to them. The audio clips are available online at www.prenhall.com/arens.

(1) Inherent risk in the consumer electronics industry.

(2) Independence rules for nonpublic clients.

Exhibit 3-1

Abernethy & Chapman

Certified Public Accountants
801 East Main Street
Richmond, Virginia 23235

July 17, 2012

Mr. Benjamin M. Rogers, President
The Lakeside Company
Box 887
Richmond, Virginia 23173

Dear Mr. Rogers:

This letter will confirm our understanding concerning the examination of the financial statements of the Lakeside Company for the year ending December 31, 2012.

We will audit the company's financial statements for the year ending December 31, 2012, for the purpose of expressing an opinion on the fairness with which they present, in all material respects, the financial position, results of operations, and cash flows in conformity with generally accepted accounting principles.

We will conduct our audit in accordance with generally accepted auditing standards. Those standards require that we obtain reasonable, rather than absolute, assurance that the financial statements are free of material misstatement, whether caused by error or fraud. Accordingly, a material misstatement may remain undetected. Also, an audit is not designed to detect error or fraud that is immaterial to the financial statements; therefore, the audit will not necessarily detect misstatements less than this material level that might exist because of error, fraudulent financial reporting, or misappropriation of assets. If, for any reason, we are unable to complete the audit or are unable to form or have not formed an opinion, we may decline to express an opinion or decline to issue a report as a result of the engagement.

Although an audit includes obtaining an understanding of internal control sufficient to plan the audit and to determine the nature, timing, and extent of audit procedures to be performed, it is not designed to provide assurance on internal control or to identify reportable conditions. However, we are responsible for ensuring that the audit committee is aware of any reportable conditions that come to our attention.

The financial statements are the responsibility of the company's management. Management is also responsible for (1) establishing and maintaining effective internal control over financial reports, (2) identifying and ensuring the company complies with the laws and regulations applicable to its activities, (3) making all financial records and related information available to us, and (4) providing to us at the conclusion of the engagement a representation letter that, among other things, will confirm management's responsibility for the preparation of the financial statements in conformity with generally accepted accounting principles, the availability of financial records and related data, the completeness and availability of all minutes of the board and committee meetings, and to the best of its knowledge and belief, the absence of fraud involving management or those employees who have a significant role in the entity's internal control.

As part of our engagement for the year ending December 31, 2012, we will also prepare the federal and state income tax returns for the Lakeside Company.

Mr. Dan Cline will be the partner in charge of all audit work. He will inform you immediately if we encounter any circumstances which could significantly affect our fee estimate of $60,000 that was discussed with you this past week. Mr. Cline has suggested a due date of February 22, 2013, for the audit report. For our work to be as efficient as possible, we understand that your staff will provide a year-end trial balance by January 17, 2013, and an interim trial balance for the first three quarters of the year by October 17, 2012. In addition, your staff will provide us with certain audit documentation, which we shall discuss with you in the next few days. Timely completion of this work will facilitate the completion of our audit.

If these specifications are in accordance with your understanding of the terms of our engagement, please sign below and return the duplicate copy of this letter to us. We appreciate the opportunity to serve you.

Yours truly,

Richard Abernethy, CPA
Abernethy and Chapman

Accepted by _____

Date _____

Exhibit 3-2

Some Common Financial Ratios

Ratio	Category	Computation	Significance
Current Ratio	Liquidity	Current Assets / Current Liabilities	Measures the short-term debt paying ability
Days to Sell Inventory	Liquidity	365 / [Cost of Goods Sold / Inventory]*	Measures the average number of days' worth of inventory that is maintained
Average Collection Period	Liquidity	365 / [Net Sales / Net Receivables]*	Measures the average number of days to collect customer accounts
Debt-to-Total Assets Ratio	Solvency	Total Liabilities / Total Assets	Measures the percentage of a company's assets financed by creditors
Times interest earned	Solvency	[Net Income + Taxes Expense + Interest Expense] / Interest Expense	Measures the ability to meet interest payments from operating income
Profit Margin	Profitability	Net Income / Net Sales	Measures the profit generated by each dollar of sales
Return on Assets	Profitability	Net Income / Total Assets*	Measures the return generated by each dollar of asset invested by the company
Return on Equity	Profitability	Net Income / Total Equity*	Measures the return generated by each dollar invested by the owners

*The denominators of these ratios are typically computed as an average balance for the period; however, the ending balance for the period is used in this case, since only two years of information are given.

Exhibit 3-3

Industry Average Ratios
Consumer Electronics Stores

LIQUIDITY:	
Current Ratio	2.16 to 1
Average Collection Period (Days)	15 days
Days to Sell Inventory	69 days
PROFITABILITY:	
Net Profit Margin	4.2%
Return on Assets	8.1%
Return on Equity	19.3%
LEVERAGE:	
Times Interest Earned	9.16 times
Debt-to-Total Assets	52.0%

Note: These ratios represent the industry averages for following four companies (ticker symbols) in the consumer electronics industry: Best Buy (BBY), Conns, Inc. (CONN), GameStop (GME), and RadioShack (RSH). The ratios were computed from financial statement data in 2009, the most recent year available at the time of publication. More recent data on some of these ratios can be computed from Yahoo! Finance (http://finance.yahoo.com).

Exhibit 3-4

Lakeside Company
INCOME STATEMENT
For Year Ending December 31, 2011

	Company Stores	Distributorships	Lakeside Totals
Sales	$5,316,000	$6,240,000	$11,556,000
Sales Returns and Discounts	(336,000)	(466,000)	(802,000)
Net Sales	4,980,000	5,774,000	10,754,000
Cost of Goods Sold	(3,216,000)	(3,654,000)	(6,870,000)
Gross Profit	1,764,000	2,120,000	3,884,000
Salaries, Commissions, Bonuses	(1,282,000)	(760,000)	(2,042,000)
Advertising and Selling Expenses	(178,000)	(254,000)	(432,000)
Rent Expense	(242,000)	(50,000)	(292,000)
Depreciation Expense	(68,000)	(24,000)	(92,000)
Other General and Admin. Expenses	(204,000)	(186,000)	(390,000)
Interest Expense	(140,000)	(88,000)	(228,000)
Income Before Income Taxes	(350,000)	758,000	408,000
Income Taxes	140,000	(304,000)	(164,000)
Net Income	(210,000)	454,000	244,000
Retained Earnings, January 1, 2011			514,000
Cash Dividends			(134,000)
Retained Earnings, December 31, 2011			$624,000

Lakeside Company
INCOME STATEMENT
For Year Ending December 31, 2010

	Company Stores	Distributorships	Lakeside Totals
Sales	$5,052,000	$5,292,000	$10,344,000
Sales Returns and Discounts	(262,000)	(388,000)	(650,000)
Net Sales	4,790,000	4,904,000	9,694,000
Cost of Goods Sold	(3,036,000)	(3,132,000)	(6,168,000)
Gross Profit	1,754,000	1,772,000	3,526,000
Salaries and Commissions	(1,162,000)	(670,000)	(1,832,000)
Advertising and Selling Expenses	(182,000)	(224,000)	(406,000)
Rent Expense	(192,000)	(36,000)	(228,000)
Depreciation Expense	(66,000)	(24,000)	(90,000)
Other General and Admin. Expenses	(162,000)	(186,000)	(348,000)
Interest Expense	(104,000)	(70,000)	(174,000)
Income Before Income Taxes	(114,000)	562,000	448,000
Income Taxes	46,000	(224,000)	(178,000)
Net Income	(68,000)	338,000	270,000
Retained Earnings, January 1, 2010			386,000
Cash Dividends			(142,000)
Retained Earnings, December 31, 2010			$514,000

Exhibit 3-5

Lakeside Company
Balance Sheet

	December 31, 2010	December 31, 2011
ASSETS		
Current Assets		
Cash	$136,000	$142,000
Accounts Receivable-Distributorship	586,000	776,000
Allowance for Doubtful Accounts	(38,000)	(48,000)
Net Accounts Receivable	548,000	728,000
Inventory(Lower of FIFO cost or market)	1,572,000	1,892,000
Total Current Assets	2,256,000	2,762,000
Land, Building, and Equipment		
Land	298,000	298,000
Building and Equipment	674,000	696,000
Accumulated Depreciation	(286,000)	(358,000)
Net Land, Build. and Equipment	686,000	636,000
Intangible Assets		
Leasehold Improvements	416,000	422,000
Accumulated Amortization	(172,000)	(192,000)
Net Leasehold Improvements	244,000	230,000
Total Assets	$3,186,000	$3,628,000
LIABILITIES AND STOCKHOLDERS' EQUITY		
Current Liabilities		
Notes Payable – Current	40,000	40,000
Notes Payable – Trade	1,098,000	1,392,000
Accounts Payable – Cypress	312,000	332,000
Accrued Exp. and Taxes Payable	212,000	270,000
Total Current Liabilities	1,662,000	2,034,000
Notes Payable – Long Term	710,000	670,000
Total Liabilities	2,372,000	2,704,000
Stockholders' Equity		
Common Stock, 10,000 shares		
issued and outstanding, $1 Par	20,000	20,000
Additional Paid-In Capital	280,000	280,000
Retained Earnings	514,000	624,000
Total Stockholders' Equity	814,000	924,000
Total Stockholders' Equity and Liabilities	3,186,000	3,628,000

Exhibit 3-6

Lakeside Company
Statement of Cash Flows
Year Ended December 31,

	2010	2011
Cash Flows from Operating Activities		
Cash Received from Customers	$9,622,000	$10,574,000
Cash Paid to Suppliers	(6,032,000)	(6,876,000)
Cash Paid for Selling Expenses	(406,000)	(432,000)
Cash Paid for G&A Expenses	(2,554,000)	(2,686,000)
Cash Paid for Interest	(174,000)	(228,000)
Cash Paid for Taxes	(172,000)	(144,000)
Net Cash Inflow from Operating Activities	284,000	208,000
Cash Flows from Investing Activities		
Purchased Land, Building and Equipment	(64,000)	(22,000)
Purchased Leasehold Improvements	(34,000)	(6,000)
Net Cash Outflow for Investing Activities	(98,000)	(28,000)
Cash Flow from Financing Activities		
Payment on Current Notes Payable	(40,000)	(40,000)
Paid Cash Dividends	(142,000)	(134,000)
Net Cash Outflow for Financing Activities	(182,000)	(174,000)
Net Increase in Cash	4,000	6,000
Cash Balance at the Beginning of the Year	132,000	136,000
Cash Balance at the End of the Year	$136,000	$142,000

Schedule of Noncash Investing and Financing Activities:

	2010	2011
Note Payable Issued to Construct a New Store	$308,000	$0

Exhibit 3-7

Lakeside Company
Trial Balance (Prepared by Client)
For the Nine Months Ended September 30, 2011 and 2012

Acct. Numbers	Account Titles	Sept. 30, 2011 Debit	Sept. 30, 2011 Credit	Sept. 30, 2012 Debit	Sept. 30, 2012 Credit
100-1	Cash - General	$57,200		$52,400	
100-2	Cash - Payroll				
100-3	Cash - Restricted	75,000		85,000	
101-1	Receivables - Distributorship	658,600		854,800	
101-2	Allowance for Doubtful Accts.		16,800		8,600
102-1	Inventory - Warehouse	1,285,000		1,524,400	
103-1	Inventory - Store 1	66,600		77,600	
103-2	Inventory - Store 2	45,400		68,800	
103-3	Inventory - Store 3	79,600		120,800	
103-4	Inventory - Store 4	34,200		49,200	
103-5	Inventory - Store 5	69,800		68,200	
103-6	Inventory - Store 6	43,800		49,800	
110-1	Land	298,000		298,000	
111-1	Building - Warehouse/Office	327,000		327,000	
111-6	Building - Store 6	256,800		256,800	
112-1	Acc. Dep. - Warehouse/Office		226,000		251,200
112-6	Acc. Dep. - Store 6		59,200		70,800
115-1	Equipment	57,800		62,200	
116-1	Acc. Dep. - Equipment		24,400		33,200
120-1	Trucks and Vehicles	54,400		54,400	
121-1	Acc. Dep. - Trucks & Vehicles		36,200		45,000
125-1	Leasehold Improvements	422,000		422,000	
126-1	Acc. Amort.- Leasehold Improve.		188,000		210,000
200-1	Bank Credit Line - Federal First Bank		836,200		823,600
200-1	Bank Credit Line - Security National Bank		648,200		756,200
210-1	Accounts Payable - Cypress		323,200		413,400
220-1	Accrued Expenses Payable				
220-2	Income Taxes Payable				
220-3	Payroll Taxes Payable		8,200		12,400
220-4	Sales Taxes Payable		37,200		40,400
230-1	Estimated Bonus Liability		12,000		39,000
240-1	Notes Payable - Current		40,000		40,000
240-2	Notes Payable - Long-Term		680,000		780,000
300-1	Common Stock		20,000		20,000
310-1	Additional Paid-In-Capital		280,000		280,000
400-1	Retained Earnings		514,000		624,000
410-1	Dividends	97,400		62,800	
500-1	Sales - Store 1		547,000		639,800
500-2	Sales - Store 2		795,600		797,800
500-3	Sales - Store 3		472,200		917,600
500-4	Sales - Store 4		484,600		530,800
500-5	Sales - Store 5		746,000		729,200
500-6	Sales - Store 6		221,600		242,400
510-1	Sales - District A		648,400		736,200
510-2	Sales - District B		829,600		888,000

Acct. Numbers	Account Titles	Sept. 30, 2011 Debit	Sept. 30, 2011 Credit	Sept. 30, 2012 Debit	Sept. 30, 2012 Credit
510-3	Sales - District C		785,000		831,400
510-4	Sales - District D		661,600		809,600
510-5	Sales - District E		677,600		690,400
510-6	Sales - District F		848,800		939,800
520-1	Sales Returns - Stores	200,800		346,800	
520-2	Sales Returns -Distributorship	311,400		464,000	
525-1	Discounts - Distributorship	31,200		29,600	
550-1	Cost of Goods Sold - Store 1	325,200		370,600	
550-2	Cost of Goods Sold - Store 2	478,600		456,800	
550-3	Cost of Goods Sold - Store 3	276,400		462,000	
550-4	Cost of Goods Sold - Store 4	274,400		304,800	
550-5	Cost of Goods Sold - Store 5	458,000		436,000	
550-6	Cost of Goods Sold - Store 6	136,200		147,600	
555-1	Cost of Goods Sold-Distributor	2,576,800		2,818,200	
580-1	Salary Expense - Store 1	90,400		102,400	
580-2	Salary Expense - Store 2	118,400		118,600	
580-3	Salary Expense - Store 3	78,600		80,800	
580-4	Salary Expense - Store 4	77,200		82,400	
580-5	Salary Expense - Store 5	109,600		110,200	
580-6	Salary Expense - Store 6	64,600		64,400	
585-1	Estimated Bonus Expense	12,000		39,000	
590-1	Sales Commissions - District A	37,200		41,800	
590-2	Sales Commissions - District B	47,800		50,800	
590-3	Sales Commissions - District C	45,200		47,200	
590-4	Sales Commissions - District D	38,000		54,000	
590-5	Sales Commissions - District E	39,000		38,800	
590-6	Sales Commissions - District F	48,800		53,200	
595-1	Admin. And Warehouse Salaries	550,800		607,200	
598-1	Payroll Taxes Expense	81,400		89,800	
600-1	Advertising Expense - Stores	133,400		128,400	
600-2	Advertising Exp - Distributor	18,200		15,000	
605-1	Travel Expenses - Salesmen	132,400		149,800	
610-1	Freight-Out	39,600		50,600	
615-1	Rent Expense - Stores	210,400		229,400	
615-2	Rent Expense - Vehicles	35,200		31,200	
615-3	Rent Expense - Equipment	12,200		9,400	
616-1	Intracompany Rent - Store 6		24,000		24,000
620-1	Depreciation Expense	75,800		76,400	
625-1	Computer & Accounting Services	20,400		25,200	
630-1	Legal and Auditing Expenses	21,400		18,200	
640-1	Repairs and Maintenance	38,200		97,800	
645-1	Supplies Expense	10,200		8,600	
650-1	Utilities Expense	89,200		72,800	
660-1	Bad Debt Expense				
670-1	Property Tax Expense	26,200		42,200	
680-1	Other Miscellaneous Expenses	79,800		67,200	
690-1	Interest Expense	162,400		178,200	
695-1	Income Tax Expense	150,000		184,000	
800-1	Gain on Sale of Fixed Asset				28,000
	TOTALS	$11,691,600	$11,691,600	$13,244,200	$13,244,200

Exhibit 3-8
Abernethy and Chapman—Overall Inherent Risk Level

Client: _____

Balance Sheet Date: _____

Prepared by: _____

Inherent risk (IR) is a measure of the susceptibility of material misstatement before considering the effectiveness of the internal control. Determine the appropriate level of inherent risk for the audit engagement as a whole, using qualitative terms (check high, moderate or low inherent risk). Complete the following table.

Factor	Discussion	Low	Moderate	High
Nature of client's business	Consumer electronics industry is subject to swings in the economy and is very competitive.			X
Results of previous audits				
Initial versus repeat engagement				
Quantity of related party transactions				
Quantity of non-routine transactions				
Quantity of estimates and judgment required for accounts				
Potential for fraudulent financial reporting (fraud risk factors)				
Potential for misappropriation of assets (fraud risk factors)				
Other factors (list)				
Other factors (list)				
Conclusion: Overall inherent risk level	Discussion for overall level is below.			

Discussion: Discuss how you arrived at this overall level of inherent risk,

32

The Lakeside Company:
Auditing Cases

4. ASSESSING CONTROL RISK

The CPA firm of Abernethy and Chapman was hired during the summer of 2012 to audit the financial statements of the Lakeside Company for the year ending December 31, 2012. Even though the year-end was nearly six months away, the firm began its preparation almost immediately.

Wallace Andrews, a manager, and Art Heyman, a staff accountant, both with Abernethy and Chapman, spent a number of days doing preliminary analyses at Lakeside's headquarters. During this time, they also visited King and Company to review the audit documentation created during previous audits. Andrews and Heyman were looking for information that would assist in the assessments of both inherent risk and control risk.

In looking at the predecessor auditors' documentation, Heyman was assigned to study the permanent file to learn more about the various accounting systems and internal control features that were in place at the Lakeside Company. While examining these documents, Heyman discovered an organization chart that King and Company had drawn to represent the client's internal control (see Exhibit 4-1). He also found the symbols used by the previous auditors in flowcharting the company's various systems (see Exhibit 4-2).

Heyman next came to a section of the permanent file entitled "Revenue and Cash Receipts Cycle—Distributorship." Apparently, two people performed this portion of the audit work originally. The "Revenue Recognition" function had been described in narrative form (see Exhibit 4-3); whereas, the "Cash Receipts" section of the company was captured in flowchart form (see Exhibit 4-4). Heyman analyzed both of these systems in detail to familiarize himself with the organization and operations of the Lakeside Company.

After finishing the initial investigation of Lakeside, Andrews and Heyman held a discussion with Dan Cline, the audit partner who had been placed in charge of the actual engagement. This group met to discuss their understanding of the client's internal control, a procedure necessary for audit planning purposes. They wanted to make a preliminary assessment of control risk, which is the auditor's expectation that a material misstatement would not be prevented or detected on a timely basis by Lakeside's internal control.

The auditor's evaluation of control risk has a significant impact on the nature, timing, and extent of substantive auditing procedures. Thus, this assessment is made early in the examination. For example, if the auditors assume the maximum control risk, then the auditors will likely perform more extensive substantive tests using more experienced personnel. Conversely, if control risk is judged to be below the maximum level, the auditor may reduce the overall audit time and effort. However, to justify a lower assessment of control risk, additional tests of the controls are necessary. After identifying specific client policies and procedures that could prevent material misstatements, the auditors have to verify both the design of these controls and their effectiveness.

As part of the preliminary assessment of control risk, the auditor must come to an understanding of the five components of internal control. To focus attention on the five areas, Cline posed several questions to Andrews and Heyman:

* Has Lakeside established the proper environment for strong internal control? Is management aware of the importance of internal control? Does management work to ensure that internal control is constantly functioning in an appropriate fashion?
* Does the company have a risk assessment policy that identifies and analyzes relevant risks to achievement of its objectives? Does it have a policy for determining how these risks should be managed?
* Has the company established control activities, policies, and procedures such as the use of adequate documents? Do transactions have to be authorized? Are duties properly segregated to prevent irregularities?
* Are the company's information and communication systems appropriately designed in order to allow for the proper identification, capture, and exchange of information in a form and time frame that enable people to carry out their responsibilities?
* Does the company have a process that monitors the quality of internal control performance over time?

DISCUSSION QUESTIONS

(1) What kinds of information should Andrews and Heyman have gathered during the preliminary stage of this audit in order to answer Cline's questions about the internal control? What sources are available to the auditors to help understand the client's internal control and assess its control risk?

(2) From the information provided to this point (including Exhibits 4-3 and 4-4), what answers can be given to Cline's questions? Mention the strengths as well as any weaknesses that have been found that will have a bearing on the auditor's assessment of control risk.

(3) After a preliminary assessment has been made of Lakeside's control risk, what possible actions can be taken by the auditors?

(4) If the preliminary assessment of control risk indicates that the risk may be below the maximum level and that assessment would reduce overall audit time and effort, then the auditor must test those controls further to determine the appropriateness of

their design and effectiveness. How is this testing of controls carried out in an audit?

(5) While evaluating an internal control system, the auditor may discover a personal problem which can lead to a dysfunction in the system. For example, assume that when Art Heyman, the staff auditor, is sitting at Ms. Luck's desk, he sees a picture of Stan Wisdon. In addition, she volunteers that "a recent trip to Las Vegas with Stan" was a disaster. "Stan, who can barely pay his bills as it is, shouldn't have lost all that money. He is going to have to sell his car, I guess." What should Art Heyman do in this situation? Discuss the auditor's options.

EXERCISES

(1) To gain an understanding of the client's present accounting systems, the firm of Abernethy and Chapman has a policy that all systems must be recorded in either a memo (i.e., narrative) format or a flowchart format. By using these formats, staff members are able to achieve a more effective and a more efficient understanding of the design of each system.

   a) Based on Exhibit 4-3 (a memo explanation of the Revenue Recognition section of the Revenue and Cash Receipts cycle), prepare a flowchart to provide a graphic display of this system. Use the flowchart symbols that appear in Exhibit 4-2. [Case4-1a.doc or CASE4.xls]

   b) Analyze Exhibit 4-4 (a flowchart representation of the Cash Receipts procedures), and prepare a written memorandum to accompany and explain this particular system. That is, convert the flowchart to a narrative description. [Case4-1b.doc]

(2) At the firm of Abernethy and Chapman, after the memo and flowchart have been prepared, a preliminary analysis is made of the internal control policies and procedures found in the system. The auditor is searching for weaknesses within the structure of the system as well as any particularly strong features that would reduce control risk. [Case4-2.doc].

   a) To assist the auditor in evaluating a system, Abernethy and Chapman utilizes the internal control questionnaire presented in Exhibit 4-5. Complete this document based on the flowchart in Exhibit 4-4, representing the Cash Receipts section of the Revenue and Cash Receipts cycle.

   b) Abernethy and Chapman use a Control Matrix to establish the existence of controls related to each audit objective. Complete the Control Risk Matrix in

Exhibit 4-6. Be especially careful to note any internal control weaknesses or strengths that may be indicated. The first item has been completed for you.

(3)　　Rogers has stated that he wants the auditing firm to help improve Lakeside's accounting systems. Exhibit 4-3 identifies the revenue recognition procedures currently used in connection with distributorship sales. List the improvements that could be made to this system. [Case4-3.doc]

APPLY YOUR RESEARCH

Use library resources such as searchable databases to research the following topic.

(1)　　Assume that an auditing firm has assessed the control risk of a new client to be below the maximum. Write a report describing the factors that could have led to this judgment. Also, indicate the various effects that this evaluation could have on the audit testing process, including tests of controls and substantive tests.

CONSULTING PARTNER REVIEW

Bob Zimmerman, the consulting partner on the Lakeside engagement, is concerned about the following issues and would like for you to respond to them. The audio clips are available online at www.prenhall.com/arens.

(1)　　Documenting the auditor's understanding of a system.
(2)　　Are tests of controls really necessary?

THE IMPACT OF SARBANES-OXLEY

(1)　　Lakeside's consideration of an initial public offering would require significant changes in Lakeside's organizational structure and governance, including the structure and operation of the board of directors and the need to assess the functioning of the company's internal control systems. Discuss these topics and make specific recommendations to Lakeside.

(2)　　Discuss the assessment of control risk for audit clients that are public companies. If Lakeside were to become a public company, what impact would that have on Abernethy and Chapman's assessment of Lakeside's control risk and the evaluation of internal control?

36

Exhibit 4-1
Lakeside Company
Organization Chart

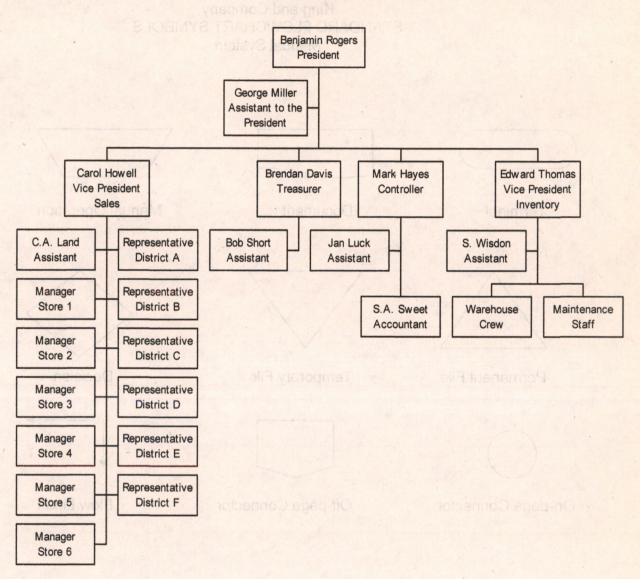

<u>Exhibit 4-2</u>

King and Company
STANDARD FLOWCHART SYMBOLS
Manual System

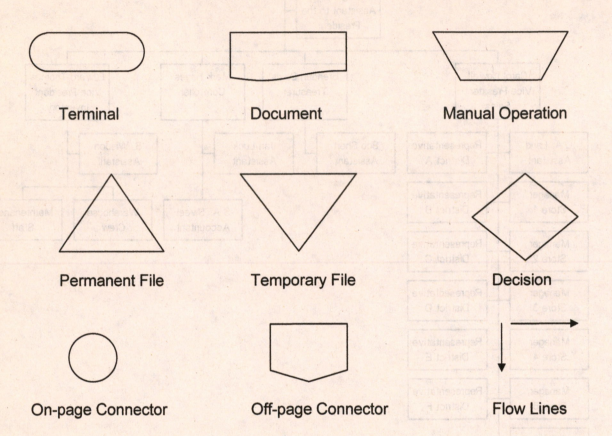

| Terminal | Document | Manual Operation |

| Permanent File | Temporary File | Decision |

| On-page Connector | Off-page Connector | Flow Lines |

Exhibit 4-3

CLIENT COMPANY: Lakeside Company

SYSTEM: Revenue and Cash Receipts Cycle – Distributorship

MEMO PREPARATION: Horace Clarke – December 2, 2011

SYSTEM REVIEW AND UPDATE:

Part A - Revenue Recognition - Distributorship

All distributorship sales are made by telephone. Either the customer or a Lakeside representative calls in each order. The Sales Division immediately records the incoming data on a prenumbered invoice, which serves initially as a sales order form. This document is prepared in five copies, with the last three being retained by the Sales Division in a temporary file by invoice number. The first copy is sent to Stan Wisdon, in the Inventory Department, who verifies the availability of the purchased items. If the merchandise is in the warehouse, it can be sent out almost immediately. However, if any items must be ordered from Cypress, the waiting time may be as long as three weeks. Wisdon estimates the ship-out date, completes and initials the sales invoice, and returns it to the Sales Division.

The second copy of the sales invoice goes to George Miller, assistant to the president. Miller maintains the accounts receivable subsidiary ledger. He also keeps a list of approved customers with maximum credit limits. However, acceptance of new customers and changes in available credit are decisions made solely by Mr. Rogers, the president. Before approving any sale, Miller checks the current age of the customer's accounts receivable balance. If the store is on the approved list, is under the credit limitation, and has no overdue balances, Miller initials the sales invoice and returns it to the Sales Division. If, for any reason, Miller cannot approve the sale, the invoice is forwarded to Rogers, who reviews all pertinent information. He then makes a final decision as to whether to accept or reject the order. Rogers indicates his decision on the invoice and forwards it to the Sales Division. If the order is rejected, the customer is contacted and all copies of the sales invoice are attached and placed in a permanent file by invoice number.

Exhibit 4-3 (Continued)

For approved orders, the Sales Division matches all five copies of the sales invoice. The approximate shipping date is indicated on the fifth copy and mailed to the customer as a confirmation. The first copy is initialed by C. A. Land in the Sales Division and returned to Wisdon in the Inventory Department as approval for making the shipment. The other three copies of the sales invoice are stamped "Approved" and remain in the Sales Division in a temporary file by invoice number.

Upon receiving the approved sales invoice, the Inventory Department packs and ships the merchandise, and Wisdon prepares a five-copy bill of lading. One copy is included with the shipment, while the second copy is mailed to the customer. The third copy is routed to the Controller's Office. The fourth copy of the bill of lading goes to the Sales Division, with the final copy being retained by the Inventory Department. It is stapled to the first copy of the sales invoice and placed in a permanent file, by bill of lading number.

When the third copy of the bill of lading is received by Ms. Luck in the Controller's Office, the quantity of inventory, its description, the bill of lading number, and the date of shipment are recorded in an inventory sales journal. Having entered the appropriate information, Luck places the bill of lading in a temporary file by sales invoice number, which has been manually recorded on the document. Lakeside uses the services of an outside computer center to maintain a perpetual inventory record. At the end of each week, Luck forwards information on all sales and purchases to the center, which then processes the data and returns updated records to the company.

When the fourth copy of the bill of lading is received in the Sales Division, Land matches it with the three approved copies of the sales invoice. He compares the quantity and description of the order with the items that were shipped. If they agree, he prices each sale from an updated price list that is maintained by the Sales Division. The sales invoices are then extended, footed, and the due date is added. The fourth copy of the bill of lading is attached to the second copy of the sales invoice and filed in a temporary file by due date. The third copy of the approved sales invoice is sent to Miller, assistant to the president, while the fourth copy goes to the Controller's Office. Miller uses his copy to update the accounts receivable subsidiary ledger and then files the sales invoice in a permanent file by customer name. The Controller's Office matches the sales invoice to the bill of lading, verifies the pricing against an updated price list, and mathematically checks the extensions and footings.

Exhibit 4-3 (Continued)

The sales invoice is then recorded in the Sales Journal as a debit to Accounts Receivable and a credit to Sales. Sales figures are also classified by geographic district so that commissions can be appropriately accrued. Lakeside representatives receive a percentage of every sale made within a specified territory. After the sale is recorded, the bill of lading is placed in a permanent file by customer name. The controller then mails the sales invoice to inform the customer of the amount payable, the due date, and the discount terms. According to the invoice, payment should be made by check (payable to "Lakeside Company"). The customer is also asked to return the bottom portion of the sales invoice, which indicates the customer's name, the sales invoice number, the gross amount payable, the discount terms, and the due date.

Exhibit 4-4

Client: Lakeside Company
System: Revenue and Cash Disbursements Cycle - Distributorship Cash Receipts

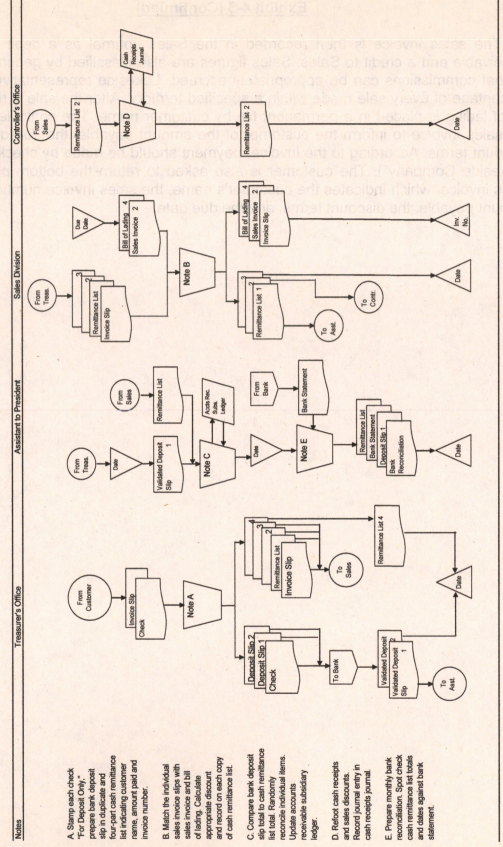

PF-12		
Prepared	JCD	9/10/12
Reviewed	JVB	11/11/12
Reviewed	EVK	12/10/12

Notes | Treasurer's Office | Assistant to President | Sales Division | Controller's Office

A. Stamp each check "For Deposit Only," prepare bank deposit slip in duplicate and four-part cash remittance list indicating customer name, amount paid and invoice number.

B. Match the individual sales invoice slips with sales invoice and bill of lading. Calculate appropriate discount and record on each copy of cash remittance list.

C. Compare bank deposit slip total to cash remittance list total. Randomly reconcile individual items. Update accounts receivable subsidiary ledger.

D. Refoot cash receipts and sales discounts. Record journal entry in cash receipts journal.

E. Prepare monthly bank reconciliation. Spot check cash remittance list totals and dates against bank statement.

42

Exhibit 4-5

Abernethy and Chapman

INTERNAL CONTROL - PRELIMINARY ANALYSIS

CLIENT: _____

SYSTEM: _____

DATE: _____

PREPARED BY:

List each document found in this system, the number of copies, and whether it is prepared internally or externally.

Answer each of the following questions. For each "No" answer, comment on whether an internal control weakness is indicated.

QUESTION	YES	NO	COMMENT
(1) Is each document within this system pre-numbered?			
(2) Is the authority for completing each document clearly delineated?			
(3) Are all documents subsequently reviewed by an independent party within the company?			
(4) Are appropriate procedures clearly spelled out for completing and reviewing each document?			

QUESTION	YES	NO	COMMENT
(5) Is the record-keeping function independent of the custody function at all points throughout the system?			
(6) Are all mathematical computations independently verified?			
(7) Does record-keeping begin at the origin of the transaction?			
(8) Are all transactions authorized?			

(9) In the space below, indicate any other specific internal control features that have been built into this system.

(10) In the space below, indicate any other specific internal control weaknesses that appear to be present in this system.

44

Exhibit 4-6

Exhibit 4-6

Abernethy and Chapman

INTERNAL CONTROL – Control Risk Matrix – Revenue Cycle
Client: Lakeside

	Revenue Transaction-Related Audit Objectives					
Internal Control	Occurrence:	Completeness:	Accuracy:	Posting and Summarization:	Classification:	Timing:
Controls	Sales orders recorded on pre-numbered forms.	L				
Deficiencies						
Assessed Control Risk						

H = *high risk*, M = *moderate risk*, L = *low risk*

Note: Each deficiency needs to be evaluated by identifying compensating controls, potential misstatements, materiality, and the effect on audit evidence.

The Lakeside Company: Auditing Cases

5. TESTS OF CONTROLS: THE REVENUE AND CASH RECEIPTS CYCLE

Carole Mitchell, a supervising senior auditor with the CPA firm of Abernethy and Chapman, has been assigned to the Lakeside Company engagement. Her primary responsibility is evidence gathering in connection with the examination of financial statements for the year ending December 31, 2012. One of the audit areas that concern Mitchell is the accounts receivable balance generated by the distributorship side of the company. On December 31, 2011, this account made up 20% of the client's total assets, and analytical procedures applied to the September 30, 2012 trial balance revealed several ominous signs relating to the current receivables in the distributorship side of the business. The average age of the outstanding accounts had jumped from 43.8 days, at September 30, 2011, to 53.0 days, as of the present September 30. Since the company sells to its customers on terms of 2/10; n/45, this calculation indicated to Mitchell that the average balance was presently overdue. In addition, the company's write-off of accounts had increased dramatically. For the first nine months of 2011, only $10,600 in receivables were judged to be bad, while $28,300 were considered uncollectible during the same period in 2012. Consequently, she viewed the inherent risk in this area to be quite high.

In the latter part of October, Mitchell discussed her findings to date with Dan Cline and Wallace Andrews, audit partner and audit manager for the engagement. At that meeting, Mitchell outlined the critical areas as she perceived them within the Lakeside examination. She also reminded Cline and Andrews of the initial brainstorming meeting and several potential issues identified [See Case 1]. She indicated that one of these potential problems was the company's accounts receivable. Because of her concern, Mitchell spent considerable time reviewing with Cline and Andrews the revenue and cash receipts cycle. All three were aware that receivables provide special opportunities for fraud, including theft and the reporting of fictitious sales.

Because of the high level of inherent risk for receivables, Cline suggested that further testing be done in hopes of reducing the control risk initially assessed in this area. Otherwise, a considerable amount of substantive testing would be required of the audit team. Consequently, Mitchell was assigned to perform extensive testing to determine if adequate control procedures and policies exist and are operating effectively. Once this test of controls is finished, a decision can be reached as to the amount of substantive testing that is necessary, and whether or not substantive procedures, such as confirming accounts receivable, can be done on an interim basis.

Cline also asked Mitchell to consider possible internal control improvements that could be recommended to Lakeside. Benjamin Rogers, the president of the company, had indicated that he wanted the systems to improve as the organization grew. Cline was well aware that relations with the client would be improved if the auditing firm could propose viable enhancements to the company's controls.

Finally, at this same meeting, the audit team decided that the existence of some of the accounts receivable balances would be confirmed directly with the Lakeside customers. Andrews suggested that interim balances as of November 30, 2012 (instead of final balances as of December 31, 2012), be confirmed unless severe internal control problems were encountered. The decision as to whether confirmations should be positive or negative, along with the specific number of accounts to be confirmed, was left to Mitchell's judgment, subject to the approval of Cline and Andrews.

Mitchell began her evaluation of internal control by identifying the control procedures incorporated within Lakeside's revenue and cash receipts cycle (see Exhibits 4-3 and 4-4). These systems record both the increases and decreases made to accounts receivable. In her opinion, a number of the procedures appear to be well designed for a company the size of Lakeside, but several problems do exist. For example, no separate credit and collection departments are maintained. Also, the limited size of the company's staff reduces the number of opportunities that are available for dividing responsibilities.

She began testing the specific control policies and procedures by seeking information that would enable her to answer control questionnaires such as the one presented in Exhibit 5-1. The CPA firm had designed each questionnaire with potential control problems in mind. Mitchell anticipated being able to complete each of these documents after a series of conferences with Lakeside employees.

On November 3, 2012, Mitchell visited the Lakeside headquarters to discuss internal control matters with several responsible officials. Her first conversation was with George Miller, assistant to the president. (Refer to Exhibits 4-3 and 4-4.)

AUDITOR: Who has access to the accounts receivable subsidiary ledger?

MILLER: I do, since I maintain the ledger, but in our company, all records are really open. I imagine that anyone who needed information could come in and look at them.

AUDITOR: How often do you age the accounts receivable?

MILLER: Only at the end of the year. However, I can easily review a specific account and determine its age at any time that I want.

AUDITOR: Is the subsidiary ledger ever tested by anyone else within the Lakeside organization?

MILLER: The independent auditors examine it at least once a year. No other testing would seem necessary.

AUDITOR: If a customer complains that an invoice is incorrect, who is responsible for investigating the matter?

MILLER: The Treasurer's office opens all mail. They have been directed to send any such complaints to me. I pull the sales invoices from my file and see what the trouble is. I personally get in touch with the customers to settle the problem.

AUDITOR: How do you verify credit approval?

MILLER: The sales representatives' file reports providing credit data gathered about potential clients. Rogers reviews this information and sets a maximum credit figure. If the account ever becomes overdue or if the customer exceeds this limit, further shipments are halted unless approval is made by Rogers.

AUDITOR: How often does Rogers approve a sale to such customers?

MILLER: I really do not know. The invoice goes directly from Rogers to the Sales Division.

AUDITOR: How are the company's sales representatives paid?

MILLER: On a percentage commission based on their total sales.

AUDITOR: Is any subsequent review made of these credit reports?

MILLER: No. If payment is made, the company is considered a good credit risk. Any customer that does not pay is a bad risk.

AUDITOR: Sales have risen; has Lakeside's credit policy been eased recently?

MILLER: Not really; the sales representatives are excellent. They have been building a good group of new customers.

AUDITOR: The average age of accounts receivable in the distributorship side of the company has increased to over 53 days, which means that the average account is currently overdue. Why is that?

MILLER: The stores that sell Cypress products are stocking up prior to Christmas. Sales are a little slow for them right now, so their payments are sometimes delayed. Our collections will be just fine again right after the Christmas rush.

AUDITOR: Why have so many receivables been written off this year?

MILLER: I am not sure. We may have been holding on to some accounts in hopes of collecting. Of course, we are also selling more; we probably generate more bad debts.

AUDITOR: How do you determine bad debt expense?

MILLER: We estimate our uncollectible accounts at the end of each year based on 0.7% of net credit sales made by the distributorship.

AUDITOR: How did Lakeside arrive at 0.7%?

MILLER: I don't know. I think we have always used that figure.

AUDITOR: How is the decision made as to which specific accounts will actually be written off as uncollectible?

MILLER: After 60 days without payment, the Sales Division pulls its copy of the sales invoice and re-bills the customer. Thirty days later, a third bill is mailed and the Sales Division notifies me. I contact the sales representative, who then puts pressure on the customer. Subsequently, the sales representative reports directly to me concerning possible payment. Based on this information, I make the decision as to whether the account is collectible. Unless an obvious problem exists, we don't even think about writing off balances until they are five or six months old.

AUDITOR: Does the Sales Division send any invoices after the third one is mailed at 90 days?

MILLER: No, any further billing is done by me.

AUDITOR:	Does Rogers or anyone else at Lakeside verify the specific receivables that are deemed uncollectible?
MILLER:	No, although Rogers has instructed me to remove companies from the credit list when their balance becomes 5 months old. Obviously, no further sales are made to these customers until payment is received.
AUDITOR:	Can inventory possibly be shipped to a customer without prior credit approval?
MILLER:	No. Either Rogers or I must initial the sales invoice and return it to the Sales Division. Without those initials, the Inventory Department is not allowed to process the order.
AUDITOR:	Does anyone verify that the invoices are correct as to prices, goods, extensions, etc.?
MILLER:	The Sales Division rechecks quantities and descriptions. I verify the prices and extensions when I receive my copy of the sales invoice. Unfortunately, by the time I get around to extending and pricing, the invoices are already out to the customers. On several occasions, we have had to rebill a customer when I discovered an error.
AUDITOR:	Could a sale be made and the invoice get lost or just not be prepared so that the customer never gets billed?
MILLER:	I certainly hope not. Approved sales invoices are filed in the Sales Division. If the bill of lading never shows up, that division will eventually check into the shipment. Subsequently, the Sales Division retains a copy of the completed sales invoice, I receive a copy, and the Controller gets a copy. If one of these copies were to get lost, the other two departments would follow up on the matter.
AUDITOR:	What verification is made of the cash discounts that are taken by customers?
MILLER:	We are very tough on that issue. Our Sales Department recalculates all discounts. They allow credit only if deserved. If a company owes us $1,000 and pays $980, then $20 is still due unless the terms of the discount have been met.
AUDITOR:	I would like to get an aged schedule of your accounts receivable as of November 30. Will that be possible?
MILLER:	It is certainly inconvenient, but I imagine we can get that done.

After talking with Miller, Carole Mitchell prepared a program to test transaction details as well as the effectiveness of the control procedures in the revenue and cash receipts cycle. The steps in this program are presented in Exhibit 5-2.

DISCUSSION QUESTIONS

(1)   What is the quality of the oral evidence ("inquiries") that Mitchell is gathering from Mr. Miller? That is, how competent is this type of evidence?

(2)   The case states that accounts receivable offer opportunities for theft. Provide several examples as to how such theft might be perpetrated.

Fraud

Fraud

(3) Cline also mentions that increased accounts receivable might indicate fictitious sales. How and why would fictitious sales be recorded?

(4) What information did Miller provide (or fail to provide) that would be troubling to an auditor?

(5) Under what conditions might the auditors omit testing the effectiveness of control procedures?

(6) The case states that inherent risk of a material misstatement of the account receivable balance is high. If the firm cannot reduce its evaluation of control risk to below the maximum level, how is planned detection risk affected? That is, what is the impact on planned detection risk of both a high level of inherent risk and a high level of control risk?

(7) What is the difference between positive and negative accounts receivable confirmations? When should one be used over the other?

(8) In selecting receivables to confirm, some accounts are normally chosen at random while others are specifically selected. What attributes indicate that a specific account receivable should be confirmed?

(9) As one testing procedure used in establishing the existence of reported amounts, the auditor will take a figure found in the financial statements and trace its components back through the various accounting records to the source documents created at the time of the original transactions. This list of forms, records, and documents leading through the accounting system is often referred to as an *audit trail*. To accumulate evidence about the Accounts Receivable total, assume that you have been assigned to substantiate a number of debit entries in Lakeside's ledger account. For example, you select a $2,800 debit entry made on July 11, 2012. What items make up the audit trail for this amount, and what information could be gathered from each? Indicate the degree of reliance the auditor should place on the data derived from these individual sources. Refer to Exhibit 4-3.

(10) Miller said that Lakeside estimates bad debts at 0.7% of sales. How did the company arrive at this 0.7% figure? Is this method reasonable? Why or why not? Why are a client's accounting estimates a particular problem area for an auditor? What testing is normally performed to corroborate accounting estimates?

(11) Should Mitchell recommend that the Accounts Receivable be confirmed as of November 30, 2012, or December 31, 2012? Why?

Ethics

(12) Has Miller made good decisions about designing the system over which he has responsibility?

EXERCISES

(1)   Exhibit 5-1 contains the questions that Mitchell is to answer concerning accounts receivable control procedures. Using this case, as well as Exhibits 4-3 and 4-4, complete this questionnaire. [Case5-1.doc]

(2)   Exhibit 5-2 is a portion of the audit program that Mitchell designed to test the operating efficiency of controls in the revenue and cash receipts cycle. For each individual test, indicate the anticipated results if the control procedure is working properly. Also, if the control is not functioning properly, what potential problems exist? Use the following format for your response: [Case5-2.doc]

Step	Anticipated Results	Potential Problem(s)
1-A	The total listed on the sales invoice should agree with the total on the sales invoice slip. In addition, evidence should be present to indicate that a Lakeside employee has already made this same comparison.	If the invoices do not agree, the possibility is raised that fictitious or misstated sales are being recorded. Lack of tangible evidence (e.g., initials) that the matching procedure has been carried out would indicate that the employees are not complying with the requirements of the system.

APPLY YOUR RESEARCH

Use library resources such as searchable databases to research the following topic.

(1)   Write a report discussing the auditor's responsibility for detecting fraud, including fraudulent financial reporting and misappropriation of assets. Also, discuss the signs that have appeared in the first five cases that should alert the auditors to potential fraud by Lakeside.

CONSULTING PARTNER REVIEW

Bob Zimmerman, the consulting partner on the Lakeside engagement, is concerned about the following issues and would like for you to respond to them. The audio clips are available online at www.prenhall.com/arens.

(1)   The impact of loosening the credit-granting policy.
(2)   Handling complaints from customers.

THE IMPACT OF SARBANES-OXLEY

(1)   As noted in Case 1, Lakeside in considering the issuance of stock to the public. Write a report discussing tests of controls for clients that are public companies compared with those that are not public companies. If Lakeside were to become a public company, what impact would that have on Abernethy and Chapman's tests of controls?

Exhibit 5-1

Abernethy and Chapman

Internal Control Questionnaire: Accounts Receivable

	Questions	Comments on Current System	Significance	Suggestions
1	Does an independent party on a regular basis reconcile the subsidiary ledger?			
2	Are appropriate, established criteria in place for writing off doubtful accounts?			
3	Are accounts to be written off properly reviewed and authorized by an independent party?			
4	Is an appropriate follow-up made on accounts that are written off?			
5	Does the company periodically re-evaluate the method in use for estimating bad accounts?			
6	Are customers billed regularly by a party separate from the subsidiary ledger?			
7	Is an independent verification made of complaints from customers concerning their bills?			
8	Was the company's policy of granting credit changed over the past year?			
9	Can a credit sale possibly be made without prior credit approval?			
10	Are credit files complete and periodically reviewed?			
11	Are invoices verified as to agreement with goods shipped and price of goods?			
12	Are extensions and footing recalculated?			
13	Are cash discounts recomputed and verified as to actual days?			
14	Can a sale possibly be made and goods shipped without an invoice being recorded or mailed?			

53

Exhibit 5-2

Abernethy and Chapman
Tests of Transactions Details and Controls
Lakeside Company Audit - Revenue and Cash Receipts Cycle

(1)   From the invoice file in the Sales Division, select five invoices at random.[1]

    a) Compare the sales invoice with the sales invoice slip.
    b) Compare the sales invoice with the bill of lading.
    c) Trace the amount of the remittance to the cash remittance list filed in the controller's office.
    d) Recompute the appropriate discount and compare the discount taken according to the cash remittance list.
    e) Verify the pricing of the invoice against an approved pricing list.
    f) Extend and foot each invoice.
    g) Trace the amount of the remittance to the validated bank deposit slip filed in the office of the assistant to the president.
    h) Trace the amount of the remittance to the account receivable subsidiary ledger.
    i) Verify that each has been initialed by an appropriate official to indicate credit approval.

(2)   From the Accounts Receivable subsidiary ledger, select three accounts at random. For each of these accounts, choose one debit entry and one credit entry.

    -For each debit entry, trace the amount to the sales invoice filed in the sales division and compare the amounts.
    -Trace the amount to the cash remittance list filed in the controller's office.
    -Trace the amount to the validated bank deposit slip filed in the treasurer's office.

(3)   Select 10 customers on the approved customer list and verify that a credit report is on file and properly completed.

(4)   Select two cash remittance lists at random. Foot the list and compare the total to the posting in the cash receipts journal.

---

[1] For illustrative purposes only. Sample sizes in practice would normally be larger than indicated here.

The Lakeside Company:
Auditing Cases

6. AUDIT PROCEDURES AND AUDIT DOCUMENTATION: TESTING THE INVENTORY PURCHASING SYSTEM

Art Heyman is employed as a staff auditor with the independent accounting firm of Abernethy and Chapman. For the first two weeks of December 2012, Heyman is assigned to the Lakeside Company examination. During this period, he is to perform a number of testing procedures designed by Carole Mitchell, in-charge auditor on the engagement. Heyman recalled that several parts of the initial risk brainstorming involved inventory and merchandise purchases. At the present time, Heyman is beginning to analyze the transactions that occur in the client's merchandise procurement system. Within this testing, he is especially interested in determining the extent to which employees comply with control procedures while carrying out various required activities. This evaluation will influence the assessment of control risk and, therefore, the nature, timing, and extent of substantive tests to be performed by the firm in this area.

Lakeside leases a perpetual inventory record accounting system from DATA Processing Systems of Richmond, an outside service organization. The initial entries are made by the Controller's division of Lakeside, and on a weekly basis the transactions are uploaded through DATA Processing Systems' website. Reports are then generated, and one copy of the current inventory balances goes to Edward Thomas, who is responsible for acquiring merchandise, while a second list is conveyed to Benjamin Rogers, president of the company. All inventory screens are also updated immediately.

Thomas analyzes the perpetual records each week, noting computerized recommendations for reorder points and noting other inventory items that appear to be nearing a low level. Based on this review, he prepares a purchase requisition to replenish Lakeside's depleted stocks. Virtually all merchandise is acquired directly from Cypress Products. The completed requisition in hard copy includes the quantity being ordered as well as a description of the needed items. This document is then forwarded to Rogers for final review. Whenever the president disagrees or questions any part of the purchase, he discusses his concern with Thomas. If they decide to make a change, the original requisition is voided and a new one completed. After approval, Rogers routes one copy of the purchase requisition to the Treasurer, a second goes to the Controller, and the final copy is returned to Thomas. The original document serves as a purchase order and is mailed to Cypress.

Periodically, Thomas must also special-order merchandise from Cypress. Customer requests are often received for inventory that is not held in stock in the Lakeside warehouse. When Thomas receives notice that specific goods are needed, a purchase requisition is immediately prepared and forwarded to Rogers for approval.

When shipments arrive at Lakeside, the members of the Inventory Department unload the merchandise and inspect each item for damage. A receiving report is prepared indicating the identity, quantity, and condition of the goods. One copy of this document goes to the Treasurer's Office, while another is routed to the Controller's Division where the inventory purchases journal is updated. Later, when the vendor invoice arrives from Cypress, a Lakeside employee stamps it so that document numbers and individual verifications can be marked directly on the form. This invoice is matched by the Treasurer's Office with the purchase requisition and the receiving report to verify agreement. The prices shown for the acquired items are compared to a master price list, and each invoice is extended and footed to establish mathematical accuracy. If all information is proper, the three documents are stapled together and placed in a due date file. On this date, the forms are removed and a check is prepared for the appropriate amount after reducing the balance for any cash discount being offered. The Treasurer uses the "Office Use" stamp and indicates the check number.

Lakeside's management makes several broad assertions regarding the inventory procurement system, as well as other systems and accounts: existence or occurrence, completeness, rights and obligations, valuation or allocation, and presentation and disclosure. Thus, Lakeside's management asserts that the inventory being reported actually exists, that the account is complete, that the inventory belongs to them, that it is properly valued, and that it is properly presented in the financial statements along with appropriate disclosures. In evaluating these assertions, Mitchell and Heyman are aware that a variety of potential problems could exist: payment might be made for goods that were never received; Lakeside could fail to pay for merchandise, thus incurring an unrecorded liability; the company may simply be paying incorrect amounts; etc. Consequently, within the audit program, Mitchell has designed audit procedures to test for the possibility of such occurrences, and, in general, to test all of the assertions made by management.

Although Heyman will perform a number of audit tests in this area, one procedure specifies the following individual steps:

* Select a date at random. From that day forward, list the amount and date of the next 12 checks found in the cash disbursements journal that are written to Cypress Products.

* Trace each of these 12 checks to the corresponding purchase invoice filed in the Treasurer's Office. Match the check information with the invoice for appropriate payment and dates.

* On each invoice, verify the presence of a physical notation indicating that a price check, extension, and footing were made by company employees.

* Re-extend and foot each invoice.

56

* Reconcile the prices charged on these invoices with the Master Price List filed in the Controller's Office.

* Locate each canceled check and match it with the corresponding invoice for appropriate amount, payee, and date.

* Examine the corresponding receiving report and purchase requisition for each of the 12 transactions. Reconcile these documents with the purchase invoice, comparing quantity and specific identification of the acquired inventory items.

* Verify that each document has been properly authorized.

Heyman has already performed the steps listed above. His work and findings are documented in the audit document presented in Exhibit 6-1. As is typical of audit documents, the one in Exhibit 6-1 contains the following typical sections: audit objectives, audit procedures, scope, comments, and audit conclusion.

The section for "audit objectives" includes the purpose of the audit testing. The "audit procedures" section describes exactly what steps the auditor performed to achieve the audit objectives. The auditor usually makes tickmarks to identify procedures performed. *Tickmarks* merely refer the reader of the audit document to a particular description, much like a footnote does. The "scope" section indicates the population from which a sample is drawn. The population can be such items as invoices, inventory listings, customer listings, and the like. The *sample size* is the number of items selected to represent the total population. For example, if the population is all purchase invoices, then an auditor selects some of these invoices as a sample for testing. The "comment" section includes a description of any unusual items the auditor finds and the auditor's resolution of these unusual items. Finally, the "audit conclusion" documents the auditor's judgment on the acceptability of the items being tested.

After completing the initial audit steps, above, Heyman's next assigned procedures are as follows:

* Choose a date at random and, from the receiving report file located in the Inventory Department, select the next 12 receiving reports.

* Review these documents for completeness and authorization.

* Verify that each acquired item was properly recorded in the inventory purchases journal.

* For each of these receiving reports, locate the corresponding vendor invoice and purchase requisition filed in the Treasurer's Office. Verify the agreement of these three documents as to quantity of goods and description of acquired merchandise.

* Verify that the requisitions have each been approved by the proper company officials.

* On the invoice, note the client's indication that prices have been checked, extended, and footed.

* Reconcile the prices on the invoice to the Master Price List found in the Controller's Division.

* Locate the canceled check for each invoice, matching the dollar amounts and recomputing any appropriate discount.

Heyman selected 12 receiving reports (Exhibit 6-2) and found the corresponding purchase requisitions (Exhibit 6-3) and vendor invoices (Exhibit 6-4). Heyman next located the canceled checks for these 12 receiving reports (Exhibit 6-5). In addition, a portion of the Master Price List distributed by Cypress has been included in the CPA firm's audit documentation (Exhibit 6-6) along with a sample page reproduced from the client's inventory purchases journal (Exhibit 6-7).

DISCUSSION QUESTIONS

(1) What control activities are evident in Lakeside's inventory procurement system? For each activity, indicate its purpose by reference to management assertions. From the auditor's perspective, what is the significance of Lakeside acquiring virtually all merchandise from Cypress Products?

(2) In the first set of testing procedures listed in this case, the auditor begins with canceled checks and then seeks supporting documentation. In the second, receiving reports are selected, and the recording of subsequent events is traced through the system. Which of the management assertions are being corroborated by each test? Why are the tests performed in these manners?

(3) The case mentions some possible purchasing and payment problems. Given the company's controls, is it possible that Lakeside might pay for goods that were never received? Is it possible that the company might fail to pay for inventory that has been received? Be specific with your answer, describing in detail the nature of the transaction that may result in the error.

(4) What is the purpose of an audit document such as the example presented in Exhibit 6-1? Does the audit document belong to Lakeside or to Abernethy and Chapman? Why?

(5) The first generally accepted auditing standard of fieldwork states that assistants, if any, are to be properly supervised. Why is this requirement necessary, and what supervision is indicated on the audit document produced in Exhibit 6-1? What other ways is it apparent that Art Heyman's work is being supervised?

(6)   What does the term *N-2* signify at the top of the audit document presented in Exhibit 6-1? Explain this numbering system.

(7)   On the audit document, Heyman has included the objective, conclusions, and scope of this testing. Why is this information important on the audit document?

(8)   The case states that audit procedures are designed by the auditor in-charge of the engagement. Are audit procedures designed separately for each audit? Do auditing firms ever use standardized audit procedures? Which is preferable for the firm's quality controls, client-specific or standardized procedures?

EXERCISES

(1)   Art Heyman performed tests of the inventory purchases and cash disbursements transactions, and he summarized the procedures performed on the audit document in Exhibit 6-1. The firm of Abernethy and Chapman has a policy that the senior (in-charge) auditor on an engagement must review and approve all audit documentation. If problems are found, the audit documents are returned to the staff auditor for appropriate revision. This review process helps to ensure that each audit document provides a clear and complete indication of the procedures that were performed and the evidence that was accumulated.

Analyze the audit document in Exhibit 6-1 as if you were the senior auditor. Prepare a list for Heyman of the problems that are present in his audit document. For each, indicate the reason that the current presentation of the audit document is not acceptable. As one example, Heyman has indicated that three exceptions were found. Are these exceptions clearly explained by the auditor along with the ultimate resolution of each problem? As another example, Heyman has included, through the use of tickmarks, a listing of audit procedures that were performed. Has he properly completed the steps listed in the audit program designed by Mitchell? [Case6-1.doc]

(2)   Details of the second part of Mitchell's audit program were described in the case. Exhibits 6-2 through 6-7 provide the client records necessary to carry out these audit procedures. Perform the tests that were outlined in the case and prepare an audit document, similar to Exhibit 6-1, to present the work and the resulting evidence. If any problems are uncovered in carrying out these procedures, simply document them on the audit document under the "comments" section. [Case6-2.doc]

(3)   Assume that Art Heyman had found one or more apparent inconsistencies during his work on this part of the audit. What would be his responsibility in addressing these problems? To whom should he inquire? What documentation should he maintain?

CONSULTING PARTNER REVIEW

Bob Zimmerman, the consulting partner on the Lakeside engagement, is concerned about the following issues and would like for you to respond to them. The audio clips are available online at www.prenhall.com/arens.

(1)   The effect of an outside computer service center

(2)   Separation of responsibilities in cash disbursements

Exhibit 6-1

Lakeside Company
Inventory Purchases and Cash Disbursements Transactions
December 31, 2012

Audit document No. N-2
Prepared by: 𝒜ℛ 12/5/12
Reviewed by: CM 12/6/12
Reviewed by: WA 12/18/12

Date	Payee	Check Number	Dollar Amount						Audit Procedures
1/9/12	Cypress Products	961	12,610.47	✓	Ø	☑	☒	∧	t u
2/3/12	Cypress Products	1480	391.05	✓	Ø	☑	☒	∧	t u C
4/1/12	Cypress Products	2322	4210.40	✓	Ø	☑	☒	∧	t u A
4/18/12	Cypress Products	2568	6069.10	✓	Ø	☑	☒	∧	t u B
5/22/12	Cypress Products	3113	841.70	✓	Ø	☑	☒	∧	t u
6/18/12	Cypress Products	3692	7018.45	✓	Ø	☑	☒	∧	t u
7/25/12	Cypress Products	4230	2292.40	✓	Ø	☑	☒	∧	t u A
8/4/12	Cypress Products	4493	667.45	✓	Ø	☑	☒	∧	t u C
9/13/12	Cypress Products	5020	318.41	✓	Ø	☑	☒	∧	t u C
10/20/12	Cypress Products	5554	15440.91	✓	Ø	☑	☒	∧	t u
11/15/12	Cypress Products	6009	8611.70	✓	Ø	☑	☒	∧	t u
12/1/12	Cypress Products	6681	2098.78	✓	Ø	☑	☒	∧	t u

Audit Objectives:

To verify that all merchandise was properly ordered and received and is for legitimate business purposes.

To verify that expenses and assets are properly valued and classified.

To verify that cash disbursements are for legitimate commitments and properly approved.

Scope:

a) Population - All purchases from Cypress Products.

b) Sample - Judgmental. Selected 12 disbursements for merchandise from Cypress from Cash Disbursement Journal.

Exhibit 6-1 (continued)

Audit Procedures:

✓   Traced to purchase invoice. Noted agreement with amount of check and payment date. Each disbursement is 3% less than the invoice amount, representing the cash discount. All discounts were recalculated.

∅   Compared invoice prices with Master Price list. All agreed except A.

☑   Examined purchase invoices for evidence that company employees verify prices, extensions, and footings. Markings or initials present in all cases.

☒   Verified mathematical accuracy of extensions and footings of invoices.

∧   Examined canceled check for amount, date, signature, endorsement and payee.

t   Examined receiving report for agreement with purchase invoice as to description and quantity. All reports were properly signed by either Thomas or Wisdon.

u   Examined purchase requisition for agreement with receiving report and invoice. Verified account code. All requisitions were properly approved except B and C.

Comments:

A   Prices on purchases of 4/1/12 and 7/25/12 do not agree with Master Price list by $200 and $360 respectively. According to Edward Thomas, the difference represents monthly purchases from Cypress at different prices than shown in the current price list. <u>Pass further testing</u>

B   Purchase requisition does not agree with receiving report for one item. Thomas indicated that replacement with a similar item was made because of stock-out. <u>Pass further testing</u>

C   Four requisitions were approved by Miller rather than Rogers. Thomas indicated that only requisitions estimated to be over $1,000 must be approved by Rogers. <u>Change system flowchart</u>   <u>Pass further testing</u>

Audit Conclusion:

Purchases and cash disbursement transactions are fairly stated in all material respects.

Exhibit 6-2

Lakeside Company Receiving Reports

Lakeside Company Receiving Report				
No. <u>3918</u>	Vendor <u>Cypress Products</u> Date <u>8/20/12</u> .		Inspected by *Jones* .	
Quantity	**Description**		**Condition**	
			Good	**Other**
5	DVD PLAYER HG87-X		X	
20	Cellular Phones IB23-D		X	
Notes:				

Lakeside Company Receiving Report				
No. <u>3919</u>	Vendor <u>Cypress Products</u> Date <u>8/21/12</u> .		Inspected by *Jones* .	
Quantity	**Description**		**Condition**	
			Good	**Other**
1	Amplifiers XX99-T		X	
Notes:				

Lakeside Company Receiving Report				
No. <u>3920</u>	Vendor <u>Cypress Products</u> Date <u>8/24/12</u> .		Inspected by	
Quantity	**Description**		**Condition**	
			Good	**Other**
1	Television BM09-H		X	
3	Receiver LM12-T		X	
2	Receiver FD23-Y		X	
Notes:				

Exhibit 6-2- Continued

Lakeside Company Receiving Report				
No. 3921	Vendor Cypress Products	Date 8/27/12	Inspected by Jones	
Quantity	**Description**		**Condition**	
			Good	**Other**
4	Speakers YG28-Y		X	
2	Shelf Audios RT 45-I		X	
2	Shelf Audios FU 87-R		X	
10	Headphones KJ32-K		X	
5	Cellular Phones BV 24-R		X	
8	CD Player XW 55-P		X	
Notes:				

Lakeside Company Receiving Report				
No. 3922	Vendor Cypress Products	Date 8/28/12	Inspected by Nance	
Quantity	**Description**		**Condition**	
			Good	**Other**
1	Television BD17-H		X	
12	Amplifier KI34-Z		X	
Notes:				

Lakeside Company Receiving Report				
No. 3923	Vendor Cypress Products	Date 9/02/12	Inspected by Jones	
Quantity	**Description**		**Condition**	
			Good	**Other**
6	CD Player NB 67-C		X	
6	CD Player XW 55-P		X	
10	CD Player RW 21-X		X	
Notes:				

Exhibit 6-2- Continued

Lakeside Company Receiving Report				
No. 3924	Vendor Cypress Products Date 9/03/12 .		Inspected by Simon .	
Quantity	Description		Condition	
			Good	Other
30	Cellular Phone BV 24-R		X	
20	Cellular Phone RA 01-0		X	
2	Speakers BF 23-G		X	
Notes:				

Lakeside Company Receiving Report				
No. 3925	Vendor Cypress Products Date 9/07/12 .		Inspected by Nance .	
Quantity	Description		Condition	
			Good	Other
1	Shelf Audio RA 69-M		X	
Notes:				

No.	Vendor _____ Date _____ .	Inspected by _____ .
Quantity	Description	Condition
	Receiving report #3926 was not on the computer	

65

Exhibit 6-2- Continued

Lakeside Company Receiving Report				
No. 3927	Vendor Cypress Products Date 9/14/12		Inspected by Nance	
Quantity	Description		Condition Good	Other
2	Amplifier BC 76-W		X	
5	Television BD 17-H		X	
6	Receiver NB 73-X		X	
2	Speakers BF 23-G		X	
2	Shelf Audio VC09-1		X	
4	CD Player TU62-T		X	
Notes:				

Lakeside Company Receiving Report				
No. 3928	Vendor Cypress Products Date 9/16/12		Inspected by Jones	
Quantity	Description		Condition Good	Other
1	Television AR 65-C		X	
20	Headphones PO 88-Q		X	
Notes:				

Lakeside Company Receiving Report				
No. 3929	Vendor Cypress Products Date 9/21/12		Inspected by Jones	
Quantity	Description		Condition Good	Other
60	Cellular Phones CB 21-S		X	
10	Receiver NB 73-X		X	
Notes:				

Exhibit 6-3

Lakeside Company Purchase Requisitions

Lakeside Company Purchase Requisition			
Vendor		**Ship To:**	
Cypress Products Box 366 Silver Spring, MD 20878		The Lakeside Company 414 Williams Street Richmond, VA 23173	
PO No. 6702	Request: *Thomas* Date: 8/9/12 Approval: *Rogers* Date: 8/10/12		
Quantity	**Description**	**Per Item Amount**	**Total Amount**
20	Cellular Phones IB23-D	88.20	1,764.00
5	DVD PLAYERs HG87-X	129.99	649.95
(For Office Use Only) Receiving Report No. 3918 Agreement With Order: OK *Judi* Purchase Invoice Dated: 8/18/12 Agreement With Invoice: ✓ BS			

Lakeside Company Purchase Requisition			
Vendor		**Ship To:**	
Cypress Products Box 366 Silver Spring, MD 20878		The Lakeside Company 414 Williams Street Richmond, VA 23173	
PO No. 6703	Request: *Wisdon* Date: 8/11/12 Approval: *Miller* Date: 8/11/12		
Quantity	**Description**	**Per Item Amount**	**Total Amount**
1	Amplifier XX 99-T	540.00	540.00
(For Office Use Only) Receiving Report No. 3919 Agreement With Order: OK *Judi* Purchase Invoice Dated: 8/19/12 Agreement With Invoice: ✓ BS			

Exhibit 6-3- Continued

Lakeside Company Purchase Requisition			
Vendor		**Ship To:**	
Cypress Products Box 366 Silver Spring, MD 20878		The Lakeside Company 414 Williams Street Richmond, VA 23173	
PO No. 6704	Request: *Thomas* Date: 8/17/12 Approval: *Rogers* Date: 8/19/12		
Quantity	**Description**	**Per Item Amount**	**Total Amount**
4	Speakers YG28-Y	274.95	1,099.80
2	Shelf Audio RT45-I	165.98	331.96
8	CD Player XW 55-P	109.98	879.84
20	Headphones KJ 32-K	9.95	199.00
5	Cellular Phone BV24-R	32.18	160.90
2	Shelf Audio FU 87-R	225.60	451.20

(For Office Use Only)
Receiving Report No.   3921
Agreement With Order: OK *Judi (Only 10 headphones received, rest on backorder)*
Purchase Invoice Dated: 8/23/12
Agreement With Invoice: ✓ BS except partial

Lakeside Company Purchase Requisition			
Vendor		**Ship To:**	
Cypress Products Box 366 Silver Spring, MD 20878		The Lakeside Company 414 Williams Street Richmond, VA 23173	
PO No. 6705	Request: *Wisdon* Date: 8/18/12 Approval: *Rogers* Date: 8/18/12		
Quantity	**Description**	**Per Item Amount**	**Total Amount**
2	Television BM09-H	812.35	1,624.70
3	Receiver LM12-T	234.76	704.28
2	Receiver FD23-Y	146.99	293.98

(For Office Use Only)
Receiving Report No.   3920
Agreement With Order: OK *Judi*
Purchase Invoice Dated: 8/22/12
Agreement With Invoice: ✓ BS

Exhibit 6-3- Continued

Lakeside Company Purchase Requisition	
Vendor	**Ship To:**
Cypress Products **Box 366** **Silver Spring, MD 20878**	**The Lakeside Company** **414 Williams Street** **Richmond, VA 23173**

| PO No.
6706 | Request: *Thomas* | Date: 8/18/12 | | |
| | Approval: *Rogers* | Date: 8/19/12 | | |

Quantity	Description	Per Item Amount	Total Amount	
12	Amplifier KI34-Z	412.88		4,954.56
1	Television BD17-H	1261.98		1,261.98

(For Office Use Only)
Receiving Report No.   3922
Agreement With Order: OK   *Judi*
Purchase Invoice Dated: 8/26/12
Agreement With Invoice: ✓ BS

Lakeside Company Purchase Requisition	
Vendor	**Ship To:**
Cypress Products **Box 366** **Silver Spring, MD 20878**	**The Lakeside Company** **414 Williams Street** **Richmond, VA 23173**

| PO No.
6707 | Request: *Thomas* | Date: 8/24/12 | | |
| | Approval: *Rogers* | Date: 8/25/12 | | |

Quantity	Description	Per Item Amount	Total Amount	
6	CD Player NB 67-C	85.32		511.92
6	CD Player XW 55-P	109.98		659.88
10	CD Player CD00-N	148.50		1,485.00

(For Office Use Only)
Receiving Report No.   3923
Agreement With Order: OK   *Judi – Cypress replaced CD00-N with RW-21X Thomas Accepts*
Purchase Invoice Dated: 8/31/12
Agreement With Invoice: ✓ BS   see Judi's note

Exhibit 6-3- Continued

Lakeside Company Purchase Requisition			
Vendor		**Ship To:**	
Cypress Products Box 366 Silver Spring, MD 20878		The Lakeside Company 414 Williams Street Richmond, VA 23173	
PO No. 6708	Request: _Thomas_ Date: 8/26/12 Approval: _Rogers_ Date: 8/26/12		
Quantity	**Description**	**Per Item Amount**	**Total Amount**
2	Speakers BF23-G	469.00	938.00
30	Cellular Phone BV 24-R	32.18	965.40
20	Cellular Phones RA 01-O	96.95	1,939.00
(For Office Use Only) Receiving Report No. 3924 Agreement With Order: OK _Judi_ Purchase Invoice Dated: 8/31/12 Agreement With Invoice: ✓ BS			

Lakeside Company Purchase Requisition			
Vendor		**Ship To:**	
Cypress Products Box 366 Silver Spring, MD 20878		The Lakeside Company 414 Williams Street Richmond, VA 23173	
PO No. 6709	Request: _Thomas_ Date: 8/26/12 Approval: _Rogers_ Date: 8/28/12		
Quantity	**Description**	**Per Item Amount**	**Total Amount**
10	Speakers KM98-G	81.40	814.00
6	Speakers VD34-L	123.40	740.40
(For Office Use Only) Receiving Report No. 3926 Agreement With Order: OK _Judi_ Purchase Invoice Dated: 9/04/12 Agreement With Invoice: ✓ BS			

Exhibit 6-3- Continued

	Lakeside Company		
	Purchase Requisition		
Vendor		**Ship To:**	

Cypress Products
Box 366
Silver Spring, MD 20878

The Lakeside Company
414 Williams Street
Richmond, VA 23173

| PO No. 6710 | Request: *Thomas* | Date: 8/28/12 | |
| | Approval: *Rogers* | Date: 8/28/12 | |

Quantity	Description	Per Item Amount	Total Amount
1	Shelf Audio RA69-M	365.00	365.00

(For Office Use Only)
Receiving Report No.   3925
Agreement With Order: OK   *Judi*
Purchase Invoice Dated: 9/03/12
Agreement With Invoice: ✓ BS

	Lakeside Company		
	Purchase Requisition		
Vendor		**Ship To:**	

Cypress Products
Box 366
Silver Spring, MD 20878

The Lakeside Company
414 Williams Street
Richmond, VA 23173

| PO No. 6711 | Request: *Thomas* | Date: 9/07/12 | |
| | Approval: *Rogers* | Date: 9/08/12 | |

Quantity	Description	Per Item Amount	Total Amount
4	CD Player NB67-C	85.32	341.28
5	Television BD 17-H	1261.98	6,309.90
2	Amplifier BC76-W	688.32	1,376.64
2	Speakers BF23-G	469.00	938.00
2	Shelf Audio VC09-I	210.34	420.68
6	Receiver NB73-X	445.70	2,674.20

(For Office Use Only)
Receiving Report No.   3927
Agreement With Order: OK   *Judi*
Purchase Invoice Dated: 9/11/12
Agreement With Invoice: ✓ BS

Exhibit 6-3- Continued

Lakeside Company Purchase Requisition	
Vendor	**Ship To:**
Cypress Products **Box 366** **Silver Spring, MD 20878**	**The Lakeside Company** **414 Williams Street** **Richmond, VA 23173**

PO No. 6712	Request: *Thomas*	Date: 9/08/12
	Approval: *Miller*	Date: 9/08/12

Quantity	Description	Per Item Amount	Total Amount
1	Television AR65-C	1318.87	1,318.87
20	Headphones PO88-Q	88.97	1,779.40

(For Office Use Only)
Receiving Report No.   3928
Agreement With Order: OK   *Judi*
Purchase Invoice Dated: 9/12/12
Agreement With Invoice: ✔ BS

Lakeside Company Purchase Requisition	
Vendor	**Ship To:**
Cypress Products **Box 366** **Silver Spring, MD 20878**	**The Lakeside Company** **414 Williams Street** **Richmond, VA 23173**

PO No. 6713	Request: *Thomas*	Date: 9/11/12
	Approval: *Rogers*	Date: 9/14/12

Quantity	Description	Per Item Amount	Total Amount
10	Receiver NB73-X	445.70	4,457.00
70	Cellular Phone CB21-S	181.18	12,682.60

(For Office Use Only)
Receiving Report No.   3929
Agreement With Order: OK   *Judi — 10 short, backordered, rest OK*
Purchase Invoice Dated: 9/18/12
Agreement With Invoice: ✔ BS see Judi's note

Exhibit 6-4

Vendor Invoices

Cypress Products
PO Box 366
Silver Spring, MD 20878

Phone: 401-555-1255
email: inv@cypress.com

Inv#   711

Date: 8/18/2012

PO No:	Terms	Ship Date	FOB
6702	3/20, N 60	8/18/2012	Silver Spring

Item	Description	QTY	Per	Amount
HG87-X	DVD Player HG87-X	5	129.99	649.95
IB23-D	Cellular Phones IB23-D	20	88.20	1764.00

Paid Ch# _3091_
OFFICE USE
Date Received: 8/25/12
Receiving: 3918
Pur Req: 6702
Priced: BS
Footed: BS
Extended: BS
Note:

		Tax if Applicable		
		Total		2,413.95

Cypress Products
PO Box 366
Silver Spring, MD 20878

Phone: 401-555-1255
email: inv@cypress.com

Inv#   802

Date: 8/19/2012

PO No:	Terms	Ship Date	FOB
6703	3/20, N 60	8/19/2012	Silver Spring

Item	Description	QTY	Per	Amount
XX99-T	Amplifier XX99-T	1	540.00	540.00

Paid Ch# _3121_
OFFICE USE
Date Received: 8/25/12
Receiving: 3919
Pur Req: 6703
Priced: BS
Footed: BS
Extended: BS
Note:

		Tax if Applicable		
		Total		540.00

Exhibit 6-4- Continued

Cypress Products
PO Box 366
Silver Spring, MD 20878

Phone: 401-555-1255
email: inv@cypress.com

Inv#   991

Date: 8/22/2012

PO No:	Terms	Ship Date	FOB
6704	3/20, N 60	8/22/2012	Silver Spring

Item	Description	QTY	Per	Amount
BM09-H	Television BM0-H	1	812.35	812.35
FD23-Y	Receiver FD23-Y	2	146.99	293.98
LM12-T	Receiver LM12-T	3	234.65	703.95

Paid Ch# ___3164___
OFFICE USE
Date Received: 8/27/12
Receiving: 3920
Pur Req: 6705
Priced: BS
Footed: BS
Extended: BS
Note:

			Tax if Applicable	
			Total	1,810.28

Cypress Products
PO Box 366
Silver Spring, MD 20878

Phone: 401-555-1255
email: inv@cypress.com

Inv#   1261

Date: 8/23/2012

PO No:	Terms	Ship Date	FOB
6705	3/20, N 60	8/23/2012	Silver Spring

Item	Description	QTY	Per	Amount
XW55-P	CD Player XW55-P	8	104.48	835.84
YG28-Y	Speakers YG28-Y	4	274.95	1,099.80
RT45-I	Shelf Audio	2	165.98	331.96
FU87-R	Shelf Audio	2	225.60	451.20
BV24-R	Cellular Phone	5	32.18	160.90
KJ32-K	Headphones	10	9.95	99.50

Paid Ch# ___3203___
OFFICE USE
Date Received: 8/29/12
Receiving: 3921
Pur Req: 6704
Priced: BS
Footed: BS
Extended: BS
Note:

			Tax if Applicable	
			Total	2,979.20

Exhibit 6-4- Continued

	Cypress Products PO Box 366 Silver Spring, MD 20878 Phone: 401-555-1255 email: inv@cypress.com			Inv# 1313 Date: 8/26/2012	

PO No:	Terms	Ship Date	FOB
6706	3/20, N 60	8/26/2012	Silver Spring

Item	Description	QTY	Per	Amount
BD17-H	Television BM17-H	1	1261.98	1261.98
KI34-Z	Amplifier KI34-Z	12	412.88	4,954.56

Paid Ch# _3251_
OFFICE USE
Date Received: _9/01/12_
Receiving: _3922_
Pur Req: _6706_
Priced: _BS_
Footed: _BS_
Extended: _BS_
Note:

Tax if Applicable

		Total	6,216.54

	Cypress Products PO Box 366 Silver Spring, MD 20878 Phone: 401-555-1255 email: inv@cypress.com			Inv# 1406 Date: 8/31/2012	

PO No:	Terms	Ship Date	FOB
6707	3/20, N 60	8/31/2012	Silver Spring

Item	Description	QTY	Per	Amount
NB67-C	CD Player NB67-C	6	85.32	511.92
XW55-P	CD Player XW55-P	6	109.98	659.88
CD00-N	CD Player CD00-N	10	148.50	1,485.00

Paid Ch# _3310_
OFFICE USE
Date Received: _9/05/12_
Receiving: _3923_
Pur Req: _6707_
Priced:
Footed:
Extended:
Note:

Tax if Applicable

		Total	2,656.80

Exhibit 6-4- Continued

Cypress Products PO Box 366 Silver Spring, MD 20878 Phone: 401-555-1255 email: inv@cypress.com			Inv# 1510 Date: 8/31/2012	
PO No:	**Terms**	**Ship Date**	**FOB**	
6708	3/20, N 60	8/31/2012	Silver Spring	

Item	Description	QTY	Per	Amount
BV24-R	Cellular Phone BV24-R	30	32.18	965.40
RA01-O	Cellular Phone RA01-O	20	92.11	1,842.20
BF23-G	Speakers BF23-G	2	469.00	938.00

Paid Ch# __3345__
OFFICE USE
Date Received: 9/06/12
Receiving: 3924
Pur Req: 6708
Priced: BB
Footed: BB
Extended: BB
Note:

	Tax if Applicable	
	Total	3,745.60

Cypress Products PO Box 366 Silver Spring, MD 20878 Phone: 401-555-1255 email: inv@cypress.com			Inv# 1616 Date: 9/03/2012	
PO No:	**Terms**	**Ship Date**	**FOB**	
6710	3/20, N 60	9/03/2012	Silver Spring	

Item	Description	QTY	Per	Amount
RA69-M	Shelf Audio RA69-M	1	365.00	365.00

Paid Ch# __3397__
OFFICE USE
Date Received: 9/09/12
Receiving: 3925
Pur Req: 6710
Priced: BB
Footed: BB
Extended: BB
Note:

	Tax if Applicable	
	Total	365.00

Exhibit 6-4- Continued

Cypress Products
PO Box 366
Silver Spring, MD 20878
Phone: 401-555-1255
email: inv@cypress.com

Inv#   1691

Date: 9/04/2012

PO No:	Terms	Ship Date	FOB
6709	3/20, N 60	9/04/2012	Silver Spring

Item	Description	QTY	Per	Amount
KM98-G	Speakers KM98-G	10	81.40	814.00
VD34-L	Speakers VD34-L	6	123.40	740.40

Paid Ch# ___3425___
OFFICE USE
Date Received: 9/10/12
Receiving: 3926
Pur Req: 6709
Priced: BS
Footed: BS
Extended: BS
Note:

	Tax if Applicable	
	Total	1,554.40

Cypress Products
PO Box 366
Silver Spring, MD 20878
Phone: 401-555-1255
email: inv@cypress.com

Inv#   1812

Date: 9/11/2012

PO No:	Terms	Ship Date	FOB
6711	3/20, N 60	9/11/2012	Silver Spring

Item	Description	QTY	Per	Amount
BC76-W	Amplifier BC76-W	2	688.32	1,376.64
BD17-H	Television BD17-H	5	1,261.98	6,309.90
NB73-X	Receiver NB73-X	6	445.70	2,674.20
BF23-G	Speakers BF23-G	2	469.00	938.00
VC09-I	Shelf Audio	2	210.34	420.68
NB67-C	CD Player	4	85.32	341.28

Paid Ch# ___3451___
OFFICE USE
Date Received: 9/17/12
Receiving: 3927
Pur Req: 6711
Priced: BS
Footed: BS
Extended: BS
Note:

	Tax if Applicable	
	Total	12,060.70

Exhibit 6-4- Continued

	Cypress Products PO Box 366 Silver Spring, MD 20878 Phone: 401-555-1255 email: inv@cypress.com		Inv#	2072 Date: 9/12/2012	

	PO No:	Terms	Ship Date	FOB
	6712	3/20, N 60	9/12/2012	Silver Spring

Item	Description	QTY	Per	Amount
AR65-C	Television AR65-C	1	1,252.93	1,252.93
PO88-Q	Headphones PO88-Q	20	88.97	1,779.40

Paid Ch# _3471_
OFFICE USE
Date Received: 9/1/12
Receiving: 3928
Pur Req: 6712
Priced: BS
Footed: BS
Extended: BS
Note:

			Tax if Applicable	
			Total	3,032.33

	Cypress Products PO Box 366 Silver Spring, MD 20878 Phone: 401-555-1255 email: inv@cypress.com		Inv#	2149 Date: 9/18/2012	

	PO No:	Terms	Ship Date	FOB
	6713	3/20, N 60	9/18/2012	Silver Spring

Item	Description	QTY	Per	Amount
NB73-X	Receiver NB73-X	10	445.70	4,457.00
CB21-S	Cellular Phone	60	181.18	10,870.80

Paid Ch# _3510_
OFFICE USE
Date Received: 9/26/12
Receiving: 3929
Pur Req: 6713
Priced: BS
Footed: BS
Extended: BS
Note:

			Tax if Applicable	
			Total	15,327.80

Exhibit 6-5
Lakeside Company Checks

The Lakeside Company		No	3091
Po Box 887			
Richmond, VA 23175		Date	9/16/2012

Pay to the
order of   Cypress Products $ 2,413.95

Two thousand four hundred thirteen and 95/100   **Dollars**

Memo: Inv# 711   **Brendan Davis**

".003091.". |:02345954|:   02 323654 01   2413.95

The Lakeside Company		No	3121
Po Box 887			
Richmond, VA 23175		Date	9/16/2012

Pay to the
order of   Cypress Products $ 523.80

Five hundred twenty three and 80/100   **Dollars**

Memo: Inv# 802   **Brendan Davis**

".003121.". |:02345954|:   02 323654 01   523.80

The Lakeside Company		No	3164
Po Box 887			
Richmond, VA 23175		Date	9/20/2012

Pay to the
order of   Cypress Products $ 1,810.28

One thousand eight hundred ten and 28/100   **Dollars**

Memo: Inv# 991   **Brendan Davis**

".003164.". |:02345954|:   02 323654 01   1810.28

Exhibit 6-5- Continued

The Lakeside Company
Po Box 887
Richmond, VA   23175

No   3203

Date   9/20/2012

Pay to the
order of   Cypress Products $ 2,860.03

Two thousand eight hundred sixty and 03/100   Dollars

Memo: Inv# 1261   Brendan Davis

".003203.". |:02345954|:   02 323654 01   2860.03

The Lakeside Company
Po Box 887
Richmond, VA   23175

No   3251

Date   9/21/2012

Pay to the
order of   Cypress Products $ 6,030.04

Six thousand thirty and 04/100   Dollars

Memo: Inv# 1313   Brendan Davis

".003251.". |:02345954|:   02 323654 01   6030.04

The Lakeside Company
Po Box 887
Richmond, VA   23175

No   3310

Date   9/28/2012

Pay to the
order of   Cypress Products $ 2,577.10

Two thousand five hundred seventy seven and 10/100   Dollars

Memo: Inv# 1406   Brendan Davis

".003310.". |:02345954|:   02 323654 01   2577.10

Exhibit 6-5- Continued

The Lakeside Company	No	3345
Po Box 887		
Richmond, VA 23175	Date	9/29/2012

Pay to the order of   Cypress Products $ 3,745.60

Three thousand seven hundred forty five and 60/100   **Dollars**

Memo: Inv# 1510   **Brendan Davis**

".003345.". |:02345954|:   02 323654 01   3745.60

The Lakeside Company	No	3397
Po Box 887		
Richmond, VA 23175	Date	9/29/2012

Pay to the order of   Cypress Products $ 354.05

Three hundred fifty four and 05/100   **Dollars**

Memo: Inv# 1616   **Brendan Davis**

".003397.". |:02345954|:   02 323654 01   354.05

The Lakeside Company	No	3425
Po Box 887		
Richmond, VA 23175	Date	9/30/2012

Pay to the order of   Cypress Products $ 1,507.77

One thousand five hundred seven and 77/100   **Dollars**

Memo: Inv# 1691   **Brendan Davis**

".003425.". |:02345954|:   02 323654 01   1507.77

Exhibit 6-5- Continued

The Lakeside Company	No 3451
Po Box 887	
Richmond, VA 23175	Date _10/10/2012_

Pay to the
order of   Cypress Products _____ $ ____11,698.88

Twelve thousand six hundred ninety eight and 88/100   **Dollars**

Memo: Inv# 1812 _____   **Brendan Davis**

".003451.". |:02345954|:   02 323654 01   11698.88

The Lakeside Company	No 3471
Po Box 887	
Richmond, VA 23175	Date _10/10/2012_

Pay to the
order of   Cypress Products _____ $ ____2,941.36

Two thousand nine hundred forty one and 36/100   **Dollars**

Memo: Inv# 2072 _____   **Brendan Davis**

".003471.". |:02345954|:   02 323654 01   2941.36

The Lakeside Company	No 3510
Po Box 887	
Richmond, VA 23175	Date _10/23/2012_

Pay to the
order of   Cypress Products _____ $ ____14,867.97

Fourteen thousand eight hundred sixty seven and 97/100   **Dollars**

Memo: Inv# 2149 _____   **Brendan Davis**

".003510.". |:02345954|:   02 323654 01   14867.97

Exhibit 6-6

Cypress Products

MASTER PRICE LIST - PARTIAL
2012

AMPLIFIERS			SPEAKERS & SURROUND		
Model	XY76-R	219.95	Model	WB11-T	56.75
	KZ54-T	269.99		KM98-G	81.40
	KI34-Z	412.88		VD34-L	123.40
	XX99-T	540.00		YG28-Y	274.95
	BC76-W	688.32		BF23-G	469.00

TELEVISIONS			SHELF AUDIO		
Model	IU76-R	285.00	Model	XZ23-U	130.00
	SA36-H	366.00		RT45-I	165.98
	JB45-H	481.87		VC09-I	210.34
	BM09-H	812.35		FU87-R	225.60
	BD17-H	1261.98		AB15-M	256.98
	AR65-C	1318.87		ND21-L	285.50
				JH88-A	324.00

DVD and BR PLAYERS				RA69-M	365.00
Model	CB90-G	99.99			
	HG87-X	129.99	CD PLAYERS		
	MN78-Z	139.99	Model	TU62-T	61.00
	DS45-W	189.99		NB67-C	85.32
	CZ55-H	495.00		XW55-P	109.98
				CD00-N	148.50
				RW21-X	165.90

HEADPHONES				PH69-D	251.00
Model	KJ32-K	9.95			
	UH76-E	15.95	PORTABLE MEDIA PLAYERS		
	BX08-W	35.90	Model	CL28-S	109.60
	PO88-Q	88.97		TL95-R	207.10
				RX04-L	285.99

CELLULAR AND SMART PHONES		
Model	RA75-L	21.98
	BV24-R	32.18
	ZN56-M	54.99
	IB23-D	88.20
	RA01-O	96.95
	CA35-T	120.00
	CB21-S	181.18

RECEIVERS		
Model	FD23-Y	146.99
	LM12-T	234.65
	JB43-A	319.95
	NB73-X	445.70
	CS33-P	698.98

Exhibit 6-7

Lakeside Company
Inventory Purchases Journal (Partial)

Receiving Report	Date	Quantity	Identification Number
3918	8-20	20	IB23-D
		5	HG87-X
3919	8-21	1	XX99-T
3920	8-24	1	BM09-H
		3	LM12-T
		2	FD23-Y
3921	8-27	4	YG28-Y
		2	RT45-I
		2	FU87-R
		10	KJ32-K
		5	BV24-R
		8	XW55-P
3922	8-28	1	BD17-H
		12	KI34-Z
3923	9-2	6	NB67-C
		6	XW55-P
		10	RW21-X
3924	9-3	30	BV24-R
		20	RA01-O
		2	BF23-G
3925	9-7	1	RA69-M
3926	9-8	10	KM98-G
		6	VD34-L
3927	9-14	5	BC76-W
		4	BD17-H
		6	NB73-X
		2	BF23-G
		2	VC09-1
3928	9-16	1	AR65-C
		20	PO88-Q
3929	9-21	60	CB21-S
		10	NB73-X

The Lakeside Company: Auditing Cases

7. DESIGNING SUBSTANTIVE AUDIT TESTS: COMPENSATION PLANS

Carole Mitchell, supervising senior with the CPA firm of Abernethy and Chapman, is beginning to prepare the final portions of the audit program for the Lakeside Company examination. This program will serve as the guide for substantive tests to be performed on the client's account balances. Mitchell anticipates that these audit procedures will provide the firm with sufficient, competent evidence on which to base an opinion as to the fair presentation of Lakeside's 2012 financial statements.

In designing specific substantive tests for this engagement, Mitchell's judgment has been especially influenced by two factors:

(1)   The firm's assessment of inherent risk in the engagement—the possibility, without regard to internal control, that a material misstatement could occur. This evaluation was based, in part, on a review of the predecessor auditor's documentation, study of the accounting system, discussions with client personnel, analytical procedures, and knowledge of the audio equipment industry.

(2)   The firm's assessment of control risk—the possibility that a material misstatement would not be prevented or detected on a timely basis by the company's internal control structure. This evaluation was based on gaining an understanding of the control structure, identifying control policies and procedures that would potentially reduce control risk, and testing the controls on which the firm would rely in reducing substantive tests.

Having already completed audit programs for the Revenue and Cash Receipts system as well as Purchases and Cash Disbursements, Mitchell is starting to design substantive testing procedures for Lakeside's payroll balances. She is aware that, except for cost of goods sold, the payroll accounts constitute the largest expense recorded by this client. In 2011, salaries, commissions, bonuses, and payroll taxes amounted to over $1,000,000, and this figure is expected to grow by approximately 7% to 9% in 2012.

Although additional personnel are hired by Lakeside each October, November, and December to handle the Christmas rush, the company normally has 48 employees:

11   full-time salaried employees working at Lakeside's office/warehouse.

| 5 | full-time hourly employees working at Lakeside's office/warehouse. |

| 6 | full-time sales representatives paid a commission equal to 6.5% of the net sales generated in their territory. |

| 6 | full-time salaried store managers who participate in a profit-sharing bonus plan. |

| 6 | full-time salaried assistant store managers who are also included in the profit-sharing bonus arrangement. |

| 14 | part-time hourly store employees (working an average of 25 hours per week). |

Sarah Sweet, employed in the Controller's Division, monitors all of Lakeside's payroll records. Each hourly employee completes a weekly time ticket as a basis for computing gross pay. This ticket must be signed and forwarded to Sweet by the individual's immediate supervisor. In contrast, salaried employees are simply paid 1/12 of their annual salary each month, and sales representatives receive a commission based on their net sales made since the end of the previous pay period.

Sweet completes payroll records for all employees by the tenth day of each month, indicating gross wages for the prior period, payroll deductions, and net wages as well as the payroll taxes incurred by Lakeside. A copy of this information is forwarded to Mark Hayes, controller, who reviews the individual records for reasonableness. If satisfied, he signs the report and routes it to the Treasurer's Office. The payroll is paid on the 15th of every month. On that morning, the Treasurer, Brendan Davis, prepares one check to transfer the total net wages from the general cash fund to the payroll fund. Bob Short, the assistant treasurer, then writes individual payroll checks to each employee based on the balances computed by Sweet. These checks are reviewed and signed by the Treasurer, and either delivered or mailed to the employees.

Sweet also maintains all other payroll records required by federal and state laws. She periodically informs the Treasurer's Office of Lakeside's need to make payments for income tax withholding, Social Security, unemployment taxes, and other related payroll costs.

Having accumulated preliminary data about this payroll system, Mitchell knows that a balance for 2012 of approximately $1.1 million is to be reported as Lakeside's total payroll expense. She plans to corroborate the reported figure through substantive procedures. She begins by identifying potential problems that could prevent the account from being fairly stated. Although she is concerned with all of the broad assertions made by management regarding this account (namely, existence or occurrence, completeness, rights and obligations, valuation or allocation, and presentation and disclosure), she is particularly concerned with the assertions of existence and valuation. For example, she realizes that a Lakeside employee may be receiving his or her own check plus another check made out to a fictitious employee (i.e., problem of existence), or that an hourly employee might be paid for more hours than he or she actually worked (i.e., problem of valuation).

Mitchell plans to pay special attention to the profit-sharing bonus that Lakeside installed during the previous year (2011). To obtain a better understanding of this program, Mitchell talked with Benjamin Rogers, president of Lakeside. He told her that the bonus had been created in an attempt to boost lagging sales in the company's six stores. To stimulate growth, he had decided to offer an annual cash award to each manager and assistant manager based on the net income of his or her store. This bonus is 2% in 2011 and 4% thereafter of a store's gross profit after subtracting direct salary and rent expenses. The total bonus for each store is then split on a 3-to-1 ratio between the manager and assistant manager. A partially completed worksheet to compute the bonus is included in Exhibit 7-2.

DISCUSSION QUESTIONS

(1)   Mitchell seems apprehensive about the bonus system operated by Lakeside. In gathering evidence as to the fair presentation of financial statements, why would an auditor be concerned by such a profit-sharing arrangement?

(2)   Since Mitchell is now planning substantive tests, the testing of controls within the payroll system has apparently been completed. This step in the audit process seeks to ascertain that control policies and procedures are operating effectively. What specific tests of controls might Mitchell have performed in evaluating this payroll system?

(3)   Lakeside is planning to report payroll expense of approximately $1.1 million for 2012. In reporting this figure, the company's management is making assertions encompassing five broad categories: existence or occurrence, completeness, rights and obligations, valuation or allocation, and presentation and disclosure. Explain how each of these assertions relates to the payroll expense balance being reported by Lakeside and give one substantive test that can be used by Abernethy and Chapman to verify each assertion.

(4)   A number of evidence-gathering techniques, such as observation and confirmation, are available to an auditor in performing audit procedures. The specific methods of gathering evidence depend largely on the type of account in question and the judgment of the auditor. List five additional evidence-gathering techniques and indicate the relative significance and reliability of each.

(5)   Lakeside maintains a separate bank account for its payroll checks. What benefits are derived from using such a system?

(6)   As guidance in designing specific substantive tests, Mitchell is seeking to identify potential problems that might prevent the fair presentation of the client's payroll

balance. Prepare a list of these possible problems. In addition, identify a substantive test that Mitchell could perform to ascertain the actuality of each concern.

EXERCISES

(1) Paul Reubens is a new staff auditor recently hired by the firm of Abernethy and Chapman. As one of his initial assignments, he is to perform several audit procedures in the Lakeside engagement. He has already completed a set of payroll tests and prepared the audit document presented in Exhibit 7-1. The firm of Abernethy and Chapman has a policy that the senior (in-charge) auditor on an engagement must review and approve all audit documentation. If errors or problems are found, the audit documents are returned to the staff auditor for appropriate revision. This review process helps to ensure that each audit document provides a clear and complete indication of the procedures that were performed and the evidence that was accumulated.

Analyze the audit document in Exhibit 7-1 as if you were the senior auditor. Prepare a list for Reubens of the errors and problems that are present in his audit document. For each, indicate the reason that the current presentation is not acceptable. Refer to Case 6 for standard audit document content and format. [Case7-1.doc]

(2) Because Mitchell is concerned about Lakeside's bonus plan, she has decided to perform additional substantive tests of the Estimated Bonus Expense (Account #585). A worksheet is presented in Exhibit 7-2 to aid in this testing. Some of the data were "prepared by the client," but the rest of the worksheet has been given to you to complete. This means that you will have to enter sales and expense data for the nine months ending September 30, 2011 and 2012 from the trial balance in Case 3. You will also need to finish what Mitchell did not have time to complete. Display your work using proper audit documentation format. (See Case 6 for proper format). [Case7.xls]

   a)   Complete the worksheet in Exhibit 7-2.

   b)   Compare the bonus expense you calculated for the nine months ending September 30, 2011 and 2012 with the estimated amount that has been accrued by Lakeside in Account #585. What is your reaction? What would you suggest?

88

CONSULTING PARTNER REVIEW

Bob Zimmerman, the consulting partner on the Lakeside engagement, is concerned about the following issues and would like for you to respond to them. The audio clips are available online at www.prenhall.com/arens.

(1) Theft within the payroll system
(2) Observation of the distribution of payroll checks

THE IMPACT OF SARBANES-OXLEY

(1) The case assumes that tests of controls have been completed and substantive testing, in the payroll area has commenced. During the internal control evaluation and testing what options are available to the CPA to document problems and communicate their effect? Write a sample of a "material weakness" in the area of payroll internal control that would be included in the auditor's report.

Exhibit 7-1

Lakeside Company Payroll Tests

May:

Name											
David Klontz	SM	M-2	Salary	45,000/yr✓	3750-*	776-^	194-^	230-*	78-	2472-✓	692-
John Quinn	SR	M-2	Comm.	6.5% ✓	4632-*	958-^	240-^	284-*	78-	3072-✓	702-
Chad Mitchell	SC	S-1	130✓	8.40/hr✓	1092-*	204-^	52-^	66-*	56-	714-✓	699-
Brenda Guthrie	SC	M-3	132✓	8.50/hr✓	1122-*	156-^	28-	68-*	98-A	762-✓	B
Carol Howell	MAN	M-0	Salary	52,320/yr✓	4360-*	1046-^	262-^	268-*	-	2784-✓	690-
David Smith	ASM	M-1	Salary	33,600/yr✓	2800-*	594-^	148-^	172-*	-	1886-✓	703-

Sept.:

Name											
Bill Grubbs	SR	M-5	Comm.	6.5% ✓	3954-*	642-	160-^	242-*	138-	2772-✓	864-
K. Steinmuller	ASM	M-4	Salary	32,400/yr✓	2700-*	430-^	108-^	166-*	126-	1870-✓	B
Jan Luck	MAN	S-1	Salary	31,800/yr✓	2650-*	490-^	124-^	162-*	-	1874-✓	870-
John Quinn	SR	M-2	Comm.	6.5%✓	5082-*	1052-^	264-^	264-*	78-	3688-✓	878-
N. Jackson	SM	M-3	Salary	46,800/yr✓	3900-*	590-^	148-^	240-*	82-	2840-✓	869-
Katrina Baron	ASM	S-1	Salary	29,400/yr✓	2450-*	454-^	114-^	150-*	56-	1676-✓	861-

✓ Compared to time tickets
✓ Verified against company records
* Verified calculation
^ Checked against government records
✓ Verified extension

A Does not appear to agree with rate schedule.

B Canceled checks could not be found.

90

Exhibit 7-2

Lakeside Company
Account #585, Estimated Bonus Expense, for Nine Months ending September 30, 2011 and 2012

2011 Bonus Plan	Store No. 1	Store No. 2	Store No. 3	Store No. 4	Store No. 5	Store No. 6	Total
Sales							
Sales Returns	15,800	50,380	23,900	28,100	60,020	22,600	200,800
Cost of Sales							
Dir. Salary Exp.							
Rent	19,200	56,800	24,000	26,400	60,000	24,000	210,400
Bonus Basis							
x 2011 Bonus %							
BONUS EXPENSE							

2012 Bonus Plan	Store No. 1	Store No. 2	Store No. 3	Store No. 4	Store No. 5	Store No. 6	Total
Sales							
Sales Returns	24,400	59,800	99,000	44,700	96,500	22,400	346,800
Cost of Sales							
Dir. Salary Exp.							
Rent	21,000	66,000	26,400	28,000	64,000	24,000	229,400
Bonus Basis							
x 2012 Bonus %							
BONUS EXPENSE							

Notes: Lakeside makes an "imputed rent" charge to Store 6 for the purpose of determining this bonus. Sales (A/C 500); Sales Returns (Prepared by Client); Cost of Sales (A/C 550); Direct Salary Expense (A/C 580); Rent (Prepared by Client)

The Lakeside Company: Auditing Cases

8. OBSERVATION OF PHYSICAL INVENTORY COUNT

The Lakeside Company of Richmond, Virginia takes a physical count of its inventory at the end of each calendar year. The company traditionally carries out this procedure on the first Sunday in January. Inventory levels are relatively low at this time of year. Each manager and assistant manager normally counts the merchandise within his or her own store while members of Lakeside's inventory department determine the quantity at the company warehouse. Since Lakeside maintains perpetual inventory balances, the final count for every item can be reconciled to the company inventory records as of December 31. All significant variations between the quantity physically present and the perpetual records are double-checked at a later date.

The independent CPA firm of Abernethy and Chapman decides that, because of the material nature of the inventory balances, observation of the January 3, 2013 count will be required. Dan Cline, audit partner for the engagement, suggests that the firm observe the physical inventory taken at the warehouse as well as the count made at two of the company's six stores. These two stores will be selected at random. Wallace Andrews, the audit manager on this engagement, is assigned to discuss the planning of this process with members of Lakeside management. Because this year's audit is the first for Abernethy and Chapman, Cline wants assurance that the physical inventory procedures are appropriate. Thus, both he and Andrews carefully review a copy of the memo (presented in Exhibit 8-1) that is distributed to all members of the Lakeside counting team. This memo is designed to ensure that all personnel understand fully the tasks that they are to perform.

As can be seen from the memo in Exhibit 8-1, Lakeside utilizes a "tag system" for counting inventory. Prior to the actual count, the inventory is separated into groups of like items. Employees then complete and attach a pre-numbered tag (see Exhibit 8-2) to each group. This tag includes a description of the merchandise and the quantity present. Later, after the entire inventory has been counted and tagged, the lower portion of each tag is detached and returned to the Controller's Office for listing. This list provides Lakeside with a record of all merchandise presently being held. Subsequently, the Controller's Office inserts a unit cost for each of these items. The total cost is then computed by multiplying the quantity times the unit cost. These individual amounts are added to arrive at the gross cost of the January 3 ending inventory. Lakeside still has to "roll" this figure back to the December 31 balance by removing the effects of any January 1 and January 2 transactions. As the final step in this process, the December 31 adjusted total must be reduced by any discounts taken in acquiring the current merchandise. The resulting balance will be reported as the cost of Lakeside's inventory.

Carole Mitchell has been assigned by Abernethy and Chapman to observe the physical inventory taken at the client's warehouse. Prior to January 3, she reviews Lakeside's physical inventory memo (Exhibit 8-1) to provide herself with an understanding of the process being used. On that Saturday morning, Mitchell arrives just before 8:00 A.M. and begins her work by discussing the counting procedures with the Lakeside employees who are present. She then proceeds to the inventory department's files and locates all receiving reports and bills of lading for the past week. She records these document numbers and their dates as well as the quantity and description of the merchandise received and shipped.

When Mitchell returns to the actual count, she has several specific audit tasks to perform:

(1)   She verifies that the tags are consecutively numbered.

(2)   She observes and evaluates the reliability of the procedures being utilized by the client. Lakeside uses a two-person system whereby one individual counts the inventory while the other records the relevant information on the tags. Mitchell makes certain that all employees understand their tasks and are following the instructions properly.

(3)   She examines the client's inventory for any sign of damage, obsolescence, or other problems that would prevent the merchandise from being sold at normal prices.

(4)   She searches for any evidence that might disclose inventory items being held on consignment or that, for some other reason, did not belong to Lakeside.

(5)   She also searches for inventory that is hidden or overlooked in the counting process.

(6)   After all items have been counted and tagged, she records the last tag number that was used.

(7)   On a sample basis, she counts the inventory actually present to ascertain that this quantity agrees with the figure listed on the tag. She records each of these test counts in her audit documents.

(8)   She authorizes the employees to collect the inventory tags.

After Mitchell completes her inventory observation, she documents her findings in the audit document presented in Exhibit 8-3. Several days later, she receives a complete listing of the company's inventory from Lakeside. The portion relating to the warehouse count is reproduced in Exhibit 8-4. This inventory has been costed using a Master Price List furnished by Cypress Products (see Exhibit 6-6). Also, as can be seen at the bottom of

Exhibit 8-4, Lakeside has already adjusted the total count for inventory transactions occurring on January 1 and January 2 (see Exhibit 8-5). Further reduction is made for the 3% cash discount available from Cypress as well as monthly discounts offered on selected items. Thus, the physical inventory in the warehouse as of December 31, 2012, had a cost to Lakeside of $1,412,071.59. On that same date, the company's perpetual records indicated a balance of $1,425,896.25 so that a year-end reduction of $13,824.66 is necessary to reconcile the accounting records with the inventory count.

DISCUSSION QUESTIONS

(1) Why would the physical count of Lakeside's inventory produce a balance almost $14,000 below the figure indicated by the company's own perpetual records? Is this difference a material amount that warrants further investigation by Abernethy and Chapman?

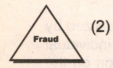

(2) Members of a company's management may occasionally attempt to overcount ending inventory. What is the rationale behind this type of irregularity? Is this potential problem especially significant in the audit of the Lakeside stores?

(3) Members of a company's management may occasionally attempt to undercount ending inventory. What is the rationale behind this type of irregularity? Is this potential problem especially significant in the audit of the Lakeside stores?

(4) Assume that a material misstatement occurs (either unintentionally or otherwise) in counting Lakeside's inventory. The problem is not discovered by Abernethy and Chapman and eventually appears within the client's financial statements. What is the CPA firm's responsibility for such misstatements?

(5) The CPA firm of Abernethy and Chapman has decided to observe the physical inventory at only two of Lakeside's six stores. Given the materiality of the inventory balance, was this decision appropriate?

(6) As part of the substantive testing of inventory balances, the auditor normally reviews the client's sales returns for the period immediately following the end of the fiscal year. What is the significance of this testing procedure?

(7) In her observation, Mitchell recorded the last inventory tag number used by Lakeside. What is the significance of this testing procedure?

(8) What actions should Mitchell have taken if she had discovered any damaged or obsolete inventory items? How would the auditor determine if the inventory is obsolete?

(9) Evaluate the effectiveness and efficiency of Lakeside's physical inventory procedures.

EXERCISES

(1) Mitchell knows that the following three audit objectives related to inventory need to be accomplished:

- verify that the physical count she observed agrees with the inventory listing shown in Exhibit 8-4,
- verify that the inventory listing (Exhibit 8-4) provides a fairly presented inventory cost balance, and
- verify that the reconciling items on Exhibit 8-5 are valid and reasonable.

She assigns these tasks to Paul Reubens, a new staff auditor recently hired by the firm of Abernethy and Chapman. Prepare a step-by-step audit program for Reubens so that he can achieve these three audit objectives. [Case8-1.doc]

(2) Carry out the audit program designed in Exercise (1) above. Prepare an audit document (similar to the one in Exhibit 6-1) to document the procedures that were performed and the evidence gathered. When specified tests cannot be completed, describe the steps that should have been taken. Indicate whether or not the $1,425,896.25 balance should be accepted as a fairly presented representation of the inventory held in Lakeside's warehouse. [Case8-2.doc]

CONSULTING PARTNER REVIEW

Bob Zimmerman, the consulting partner on the Lakeside engagement, is concerned about the following issues and would like for you to respond to them. The audio clips are available online at www.prenhall.com/arens.

(1) Valuation problems with inventory
(2) Selling on consignment

APPLY YOUR RESEARCH

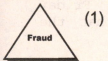

(1) Several recent accounting scandals involved revenue recognition irregularities. Identify some of these scandals, and suggest specific audit steps designed to discover these types of fraudulent activities.

Exhibit 8-1

Lakeside Company
INTERCOMPANY MEMO

TO: All Store Managers, All Assistant Store Managers,
             All Members of the Inventory Department

FROM: Edward Thomas, Vice-President

SUBJECT: Annual Physical Inventory

DATE: December 2, 2012

We will count the inventory at all of the Lakeside stores as well
as the warehouse on January 3, 2013. Each of the store managers will be
responsible for the physical inventory at their store. The inventory
department will count the merchandise here at the warehouse. You should
plan to perform the following steps:

PRELIMINARY

(1) During the week prior to the 3rd, ship out all inventory that has
     been sold so that it will not be accidentally counted.

(2) Isolate and label any inventory that does not belong to Lakeside.
     These items will include merchandise returned for repair as well
     as sold inventory that could not be shipped out at this time.

(3) Isolate and label any damaged inventory or other items where
     marketability has been impaired.

(4) Group similar inventory items. Counting will be easier and quicker
     if, for example, all radios of a particular type are already
     together.

(5) Make certain that you have enough prenumbered inventory tags.
     These tags should be picked up at the warehouse by Friday
     afternoon. You should have at least 200 tags. Verify that the
     numbers are sequential and that no numbers are missing.

(6) Inform all employees who will be assisting in the count of their
     responsibilities. Give each of these employees a copy of this memo
     and ask them to read it prior to the 3rd.

Counting Procedures

(1) Have all employees arrive by 8:00 A.M. on January 3. We normally
     assume that two people can count a store's entire inventory in
     about 4 to 6 hours. Eight people will be needed to count the

96

warehouse inventory. You may ask more employees to assist but remember that they must be paid overtime wage rates.

(2)   A member of the auditing firm of Abernethy and Chapman may be present to observe your count. If an auditor is on hand, this individual should be given full cooperation and allowed to perform any procedures considered necessary.

(3)   Divide the employees into two-member counting teams. Before the actual count begins, review all instructions with each team.

(4)   One member of each team should count the inventory while the other records the quantity, the type of item, and the Cypress serial number on a prenumbered inventory tag. The tag should then be attached at a prominent place on the inventory items. Tags must be used sequentially.

(5)   All tags should be completed in ink. If a change needs to be made to a tag, the original data should be marked out and the correction entered. The person making the alteration must initial the change. To ensure that unauthorized changes are not made, no erasures are permitted.

(6)   If any tags have to be voided, write "VOID" across the face. These tags should be saved and returned with the unused tags.

(7)   Each team is responsible for counting all inventory within the assigned areas. Any items not counted should be clearly labeled, giving the reasons for exclusion.

(8)   When a team has counted and tagged all inventory, the person in charge of the count should be informed (as well as the auditor if present).

(9)   The in-charge employee will examine the area to ensure that all merchandise is tagged. The auditor should be allowed to perform whatever tests are considered necessary. After both the in-charge employee and the auditor have completed their review, the counting team will return and remove the bottom portion of each tag.

(10) The counting team sorts the tags into numerical order making certain that all tags are present. When all tags are located, the in-charge employee should bring them directly to the company office and give them to me in the afternoon.

(11) If any problems arise, call me at the company office immediately.

Exhibit 8-2

Lakeside Company

SAMPLE - INVENTORY TAG

INVENTORY TAG

No. 101

No. 101

ITEM DESCRIPTION:

SERIAL NUMBER:

QUANTITY:

UNIT OF MEASURE:

COUNTED BY: _____

CHECKED BY: _____

Exhibit 8-3

W.P. No.	F-1
Accountant	CM
Date	1/2/2013

LAKESIDE COMPANY-RECEIVING & SHIPPING INVENTORY CUT-OFF
DECEMBER 31, 2012

I. Receiving reports (week of 12/28/2012 – 1/2/2013)

		R.R. #	Serial #	Quantity
Cellular Phones	12/28/12	3987	IB23-D	75
Speakers	12/28/12	3987	VD34-L	40
Amplifiers	12/28/12	3987	KZ54-T	50
Televisions	1/1/13	3988	JB45-H	22
Headphones	1/2/13	3989	KJ32-K	32
Portable Media Players	1/2/13	3989	RX04-L	10

II. Bills of Lading (week of 12/28/2012 – 1/2/2013)

		Shipped to	B.L.#	Serial #	Quantity
12/28/12	Televisions	Customer	6012	SA36-H	5
12/28/12	Cellular Phones	Customer	6013	ZN56-M	20
12/30/12	Amplifiers	Store 4	6014	XX99-T	5
12/30/12	Amplifiers	Store 4	6014	BC76-W	4
1/1/13	Amplifiers	Customer	6015	XY76-R	20
1/1/13	Televisions	Customer	6015	BM09-H	10
1/2/13	Shelf Audio	Customer	6016	AB15-M	20
1/2/13	Shelf Audio	Customer	6016	JH88-A	12
1/2/13	Receivers	Customer	6016	CS33-P	10
1/2/13	Televisions	Customer	6016	AR65-C	6
1/2/13	Speakers	Store 1	6017	BF23-G	8

Inventory Tag Count and Procedures

- Lakeside uses a tag system in counting inventory. Each team member appeared to understand and follow company procedures.

- Counting teams were:
  1. Stan Wisdon   2. David Stockman   3. Edward Thomas   4. Jeff Mullins
     Ralph Lewis   Ron Livingston   Chad Nance   Bob Simon

- Tags #101-300 assigned to warehouse. All tags reviewed and found to be consecutively numbered. Last tag used: #152. All tags (#101-152) were pulled and accounted for.

Exhibit 8-3 (continued)

W/P F-2
CM
1/2/2013

LAKESIDE COMPANY-PHYSICAL INVENTORY TEST COUNTS-WAREHOUSE
DECEMBER 31, 2012

Inventory items	Tag No.	Serial No.	Quantity	
Amplifiers	116	BC76-W	44	
Televisions	124	JB45-H	69	
Cellular Phones	102	CB21-S	160	
Shelf Audio	138	FU87-R	60	A
Amplifiers	130	KZ54-T	170	
Speakers	150	YG28-Y	71	
Shelf Audio	127	RA69-M	99	
CD PLAYERs	142	RW21-X	49	
Receivers	113	NB73-X	112	
Shelf Audio	126	JH88-A	77	
DVD Players	104	CZ55-H	92	
Speakers	137	BF23-G	84	
Headphones	147	PO88-Q	94	
CD PLAYERs	132	CD00-N	121	

A - Lakeside's count was adjusted from 59 to 60.

Several items did not belong to Lakeside. They had been returned for repairs or adjustment and a properly completed "Repair memo" was on hand signed by the customer and a Lakeside representative. These items did not appear to have a value of over $1000.

Audit Objective:
To gather evidence of inventory existence and to assure that it was counted accurately. To verify that unsalable merchandise is excluded and imperfect items are appropriately earmarked.

Audit Conclusion:
All items (except A above) correctly counted with no items missing or omitted. No damaged or obsolete inventory was observed in the warehouse.

Exhibit 8-4

Lakeside Company

PHYSICAL INVENTORY - WAREHOUSE

January 3, 2013   Page 1 of 2

TAG NUMBER	DESCRIPTION	SERIAL NUMBER	QUAN- TITY	COST/UNIT	TOTAL COST
101	Cellular Phones	BV24-R	141	32.18	4,537.38
102	Cellular Phones	CB21-S	160	181.18	28,988.80
103	DVD Players	CB90-G	250	99.99	24,997.50
104	DVD Players	CZ55-H	92	495.00	45,540.00
105	Cellular Phones	CA35-T	121	120.00	14,520.00
106	Receivers	JB43-A	302	319.95	96,624.90
107	Receivers	LM12-T	210	234.65	49,276.50
108	Receivers	CS33-P	24	698.98	16,775.52
109	Cellular Phones	RA01-O	253	96.95	24,528.35
110	Cellular Phones	IB23-D	243	88.20	21,432.60
111	Amplifiers	XY76-R	201	219.95	44,209.95
112	Receivers	FD23-Y	156	146.99	22,930.44
113	Receivers	NB73-X	112	445.70	49,918.40
114	Televisions	SA36-H	11	366.00	4,026.00
115	Amplifiers	XX99-T	121	540.00	65,340.00
116	Amplifiers	BC76-W	44	688.32	30,286.08
117	Televisions	AR65-C	13	1,318.87	17,145.31
118	Televisions	BD17-H	126	1,261.98	159,009.48
119	Televisions	IU76-R	90	285.00	25,650.00
120	Cellular Phones	RA75-L	234	21.98	5,143.32
121	Cellular Phones	ZN56-M	176	54.99	9,678.24
122	Speakers	VD34-L	171	123.40	21,101.40
123	Speakers	WB11-T	95	56.75	5,391.25
124	Televisions	JB45-H	69	481.87	33,249.03
125	Televisions	BM09-H	17	812.35	13,809.95
126	Shelf Audio	JH88-A	77	324.00	24,948.00
127	Shelf Audio	RA69-M	99	365.00	36,135.00
128	Shelf Audio	XZ23-U	211	130.00	27,430.00
129	Shelf Audio	VC09-I	173	210.34	36,388.82
130	Amplifiers	KZ54-T	170	269.99	45,898.30

Exhibit 8-4 (Continued)

Lakeside Company

PHYSICAL INVENTORY - WAREHOUSE

January 3, 2013   Page 2 of 2

TAG NUMBER	DESCRIPTION	SERIAL NUMBER	QUAN-TITY	COST/UNIT	TOTAL COST
131	Amplifiers	KI34-Z	40	412.88	16,515.20
132	CD Players	CD00-N	121	148.50	17,968.50
133	Shelf Audio	RT45-I	11	165.98	1,825.78
134	CD Players	PH69-D	9	251.00	2,259.00
135	Shelf Audio	ND21-L	230	285.50	65,665.00
136	Shelf Audio	AB15-M	70	256.98	17,988.60
137	Speakers	BF23-G	84	469.00	39,396.00
138	Shelf Audio	FU87-R	60	225.60	13,536.00
139	CD Players	TU62-T	174	61.00	10,614.00
140	CD Players	NB67-C	23	85.32	1,962.36
141	Headphones	BX08-W	198	35.90	7,108.20
142	CD Players	RW21-X	49	165.90	8,129.10
143	DVD Players	HG87-X	246	129.99	31,977.54
144	DVD Players	DS45-W	436	189.99	82,835.64
145	DVD Players	MN78-Z	56	139.99	7,839.44
146	CD Players	XW55-P	295	109.98	32,444.10
147	Headphones	PO88-Q	94	88.97	8,363.18
148	Headphones	KJ32-K	289	9.95	2,875.55
149	Speakers	KM98-G	240	81.40	19,536.00
150	Speakers	YG28-Y	71	274.95	19,521.45
151	Headphones	UH76-E	15	15.95	239.25
152	Portable Media Players	RX04-L	72	285.99	20,591.28

TOTAL COST OF INVENTORY-JANUARY 3, 2013-Warehouse $1,434,101.69

Exhibit 8-5

Lakeside Company

RECONCILIATION OF
PHYSICAL INVENTORY - WAREHOUSE
January 3, 2013

TOTAL COST OF INVENTORY - JANUARY 3, 2013 - WAREHOUSE	$1,434,101.69
Less: Inventory Received on January 1 and January 2 (from Receiving Reports)	(13,779.40)
Add: Inventory Shipped Out on January 1 and January 2 (from Bills of Lading)	40,205.12
TOTAL COST OF INVENTORY - DECEMBER 31, 2012 - WAREHOUSE	$1,460,527.41
Less: Adjustments for Monthly Discounts Given by Cypress	
Tag 113 - Discount $30.00 x 85 Items Purchased	(2,550.00)
Tag 121 - Discount $ 8.25 x 40 Items Purchased	(330.00)
Tag 132 - Discount $12.60 x 60 Items Purchased	(756.00)
Tag 146 - Discount $11.50 x 80 Items Purchased	(920.00)
Tag 149 - Discount $ 6.50 x 35 Items Purchased	(227.50)
SUB-TOTAL	$1,455,743.91
Less: Adjustment for 3% Cash Discount Taken on All Inventory Purchases	(43,672.32)
TOTAL ADJUSTED COST OF INVENTORY - DECEMBER 31, 2012 - WAREHOUSE	$1,412,071.59
INVENTORY IN WAREHOUSE PER PERPETUAL INVENTORY RECORDS	(1,425,896.25)
INVENTORY ADJUSTMENT (REDUCTION)	$(13,824.66)

The Lakeside Company: Auditing Cases

9. RESOLVING AUDIT PROBLEMS

Early in 2013, Wallace Andrews, manager with the CPA firm of Abernethy and Chapman, visited the headquarters of the Lakeside Company. Andrews was making a periodic review of the audit work performed to date by Carole Mitchell, Art Heyman, and Paul Reubens. He also wanted to discuss the examination with Benjamin Rogers, president of Lakeside. During every engagement, Abernethy and Chapman auditors attempt to keep the client's senior management advised of the progress being made. In addition, several matters had been brought to Andrews' attention that he felt should be discussed with Rogers.

The first of these issues concerned a major addition being made to the company warehouse. In reading the minutes of the Board of Directors' meetings (see Exhibit 9-1), Andrews had noted the Board's approval of a $220,000 expansion and renovation to this facility. Early in December, Andrews inspected the actual construction work, which was approximately one-fourth complete at that time. Then, at year-end, a bank confirmation was mailed to the Virginia Capital Security Bank, the organization financing the project (see Exhibit 9-2). The completed confirmation returned by the bank indicated that Lakeside had borrowed $100,000 to date.

When asked about the construction, Rogers described Lakeside's negotiation of a $200,000 mortgage loan to finance the expansion. The cash was to be provided to the company in four equal monthly installments beginning on November 15. According to Rogers, "This entire construction project, both the addition and the renovation, should be finished by March 1, 2013. Although we can't be sure of the total cost just yet, it should be approximately $225,000. We will use Lakeside's own funds to finance costs over and above the $200,000 loan. We borrowed the money from Virginia Capital at a 10% rate. I talked to a number of other banks and lenders but that was the best rate that was available at the time."

Several potential accounting problems involving the expansion concerned Andrews. First, he was worried that Lakeside might already be recording depreciation expense on the addition even though it was not yet in operation. Rogers assumed that the company's method of accounting was correct but suggested that Andrews discuss the handling of this matter with the controller.

Andrews also wanted to verify that Lakeside was properly capitalizing the interest costs incurred during the construction as required by *Statement 34* of the Financial

Accounting Standards Board (FASB). Rogers confessed that he knew nothing about this particular accounting pronouncement. He was virtually certain, though, that Lakeside would have expensed any interest on the debt. However, no interest charges had yet been paid or recorded in connection with the project. Rogers suggested that the audit team calculate an appropriate adjustment to capitalize this interest for the current period.

Andrews' final concern in auditing the warehouse expansion involved Lakeside's method of separating repair expenses from capitalized costs. Improper capitalization of expenses was an issue in several recent accounting scandals, and this issue was discussed during the fraud brainstorming session by the audit team. The Board of Directors' minutes had indicated that the old warehouse facility was to be repaired as part of the construction work. Andrews was interested in the procedures being used by the company to isolate these repair costs. Rogers replied that no special techniques had been incorporated to account for the construction project. As with all expenditures, except for inventory purchases, which were handled separately, invoices were "coded" by the Controller's Office upon receipt. This process required each invoice to be stamped and an account number written in to identify the appropriate debit entry for the transaction. Thus, all invoices were reviewed and classified at that time to separate capital expenditures from repair expenses. Rogers stated that his signature was also necessary on all invoices that required a payment of over $200, but he made no attempt to verify the accuracy of the account coding.

Andrews then moved the discussion to the issue of the seventh store, which Lakeside had begun operating on December 1, 2012, in Williamsburg, Virginia. Carole Mitchell had informed Andrews that Lakeside made a $21,000 payment on November 28, 2012, to Rogers Development Company, the corporation that constructed this building and was leasing it to Lakeside. She also revealed that Benjamin Rogers and his wife own Rogers Development Company. The entire $21,000 had been charged by Lakeside to a Prepaid Rent account with 1/12 of this total being subsequently reclassified to Rent Expense for the month of December. Andrews was very concerned as to whether this rental agreement constituted a capitalized lease based on the criteria established by *Statement 13* of the FASB. He was also concerned as to the possibility that Rogers Development Company might actually be a variable interest entity (also known as a *special purpose entity*) that may need to be consolidated with the Lakeside Company's financial statements.

Rogers adamantly refused to even entertain the possibility that this arrangement might be a capital lease or that Rogers Development Company might be a special purpose entity. He immediately brought out the rental contract (see Exhibit 9-3) between Lakeside and his construction company. "The agreement is for one year only. We will renegotiate on a year-by-year basis; the Board of Directors fully agrees with the handling of this matter. In addition, the price is quite reasonable for that store at that location. I even checked into this matter with a lawyer before drawing up the contract. Neither a bargain purchase option nor a transfer of ownership is included in the lease. The building has a useful life of at least 25 years; thus, the one-year contract is for a period of time less than

75% of the property's economic life. Finally, since the residual value is not guaranteed, the $21,000 payment fails to satisfy the 90% present value criterion. This lease simply does not meet any test for being a capital lease."

Andrews was quite surprised by Rogers' fervor and knowledge of this FASB Statement. Upon further questioning, the president indicated that "growth is important to me. To grow, Lakeside has to be able to borrow money and, thus, needs a good debt/equity ratio. By financing the building in this manner, the construction debt is actually mine and not that of the company. I plan to earn a reasonable return on my investment but, even more importantly, Lakeside maintains its borrowing potential. I do realize that this lease qualifies as a related-party transaction and will have to be disclosed in a note to the financial statements. However, I'm not sure that anyone actually reads those notes."

Andrews was concerned by Rogers' contentions and decided to discuss the issue with Dan Cline, the audit partner on the engagement, before taking further action. He wanted to read *Statement 13* once again to see if any guidance was offered by the pronouncement about capital leases. Andrews also wanted to review FASB *Interpretation 46* about variable interest entities. Thus, he chose to forgo additional discussion with Rogers concerning the lease and moved to his final agenda item: Lakeside's Store 6.

Store 6 first began operations in November of 2010 but had never proven successful. The previous audit firm had even qualified its opinion on Lakeside's 2011 financial statements because of Rogers' unwillingness to record or disclose the impairment of the value of the company's investment. Although sales were up slightly in 2012, the store continued to show a considerable loss after two years of operation. The adjacent shopping center was still having its own problems, with less than 60% of the available space being rented. Reviewing King and Company's workpapers disclosed that, last year, an appraisal had been obtained and set the value of the store at $150,000. Andrews believes that Store 6 is capable of generating only a marginal profit over it's expected life of twenty years. See the cash flows by store in Case 7.

When questioned, Rogers was somewhat philosophical about the situation. "We studied that market before we went into it. We felt that the location had long-range potential and we still do. When Rogers was reminded of the appraisal he was adamant, "I rejected that amount last year!" "I am not planning to sell the store. I believe that my decision to operate that store in the long-term will be a wise investment." Lakeside is not the kind of company that enters an area on an impulse and then pulls up stakes if things don't go our way at first. We can make that store a success, and we will. I wasted too much time last year arguing with King and Company over this issue. As you know, that firm is gone and the store is still at the shopping center making sales. Store 6 will be doing business for as long as Lakeside is in business. I really have nothing further to say on the matter."

DISCUSSION QUESTIONS

(1) Why would a company's principal officer not know about an important accounting pronouncement by the FASB?

(2) Why is depreciation expense not recorded until after an asset is put into use?

(3) Rogers suggested that Abernethy and Chapman calculate the amount of interest that should be capitalized this year for the construction project. Since the financial statements are the responsibility of management, is this action appropriate for an audit engagement?

(4) What should Andrews do now concerning the lease arrangement that has been created for the seventh store? Will Lakeside's financial statements be fairly presented if this lease is reported as an operating lease rather than a capitalized lease? Is inclusion within the notes to the financial statements an adequate way of reporting this lease?

(5) Why are related party transactions separately disclosed in financial statement notes?

(6) When Rogers made reference to the firing of King and Company, was he issuing a threat to the current auditors? If so, how should Abernethy and Chapman react to such a threat?

EXERCISE

(1) Following his discussion with Rogers, Andrews talked briefly with Carole Mitchell concerning the warehouse expansion. She indicated that Art Heyman had already prepared an analysis of the Repairs and Maintenance account (see Exhibit 9-4). In addition, based on the debits to the Warehouse account (see Exhibit 9-5) he had located the invoices substantiating the capitalized transactions (see Exhibit 9-6). The audit team discovered two other related invoices (see Exhibit 9-7) while reviewing the invoices received by Lakeside subsequent to the end of 2012.

Perform the necessary steps to test the warehouse account (#111-1) and document your procedures on an audit document similar to the one in Exhibit 9-4. Indicate and prepare on the audit document any proposed correcting entries that are needed to ensure fair presentation of this financial information. [Case9-1.doc]

(2) Despite Rogers' assurances, Store 6 could still be closed down, resulting in a large loss to Lakeside. The audit opinion was qualified in the previous year, and the situation has not changed significantly. Perform an impairment test given the

information available. What should Abernethy and Chapman do now in connection with the uncertainty involved with Store 6? Should Abernethy and Chapman give a similar opinion this year to protect the firm from potential liability? (Hint: information for this question makes use of information from Case 3 and Case 7).

APPLY YOUR RESEARCH

Use library resources such as searchable databases to research the following topic.

(1)   The Lakeside Company is leasing its Store 7 from Rogers Development Company, a corporation owned by the president of Lakeside and his spouse. Write a report discussing the issue of variable interest entities (sometimes called *special purpose entities*"). Does Rogers Development Company meet the definition of an variable interest entity? If so, should it be consolidated into the financial statements of Lakeside? (Hint: Read *Interpretation No. 46* by the FASB at www.fasb.org).

CONSULTING PARTNER REVIEW

Bob Zimmerman, the consulting partner on the Lakeside engagement, is concerned about the following issues and would like for you to respond to them. The audio clips are available online at www.prenhall.com/arens.

(1)   Computing interest to be capitalized
(2)   Net income and asset impairment

SARBANES-OXLEY

(1)   The Sarbanes-Oxley legislation raised the expectations on the oversight provided by the board of directors and established the role of the "financial expert." How would these expanded responsibilities affect the financial accounting questions that played a significant part in Case 9?

(2)   Under Sarbanes-Oxley, management can no longer claim to be unaware of its financial reporting system. In this case, how do the answers provided by Rogers relate to his anticipated plan to take his company public?

Exhibit 9-1

Lakeside Company
MINUTES - BOARD OF DIRECTORS' MEETING
September 1, 2012

Meeting was called to order at 1:00 P.M.
Members present: Benjamin Rogers, Scott Arnold, Steve Reese, and Roberta Verga
Members absent: None

Rogers distributed Lakeside's interim financial information for the first two quarters of 2012 and discussed the major changes in results from the previous year. Questions followed concerning specific revenue and expense items. Discussion centered on methods for increasing store sales, especially at Store 6. Rogers stated that he was confident the new bonus incentive system would generate additional sales by encouraging the management of each store to be more aggressive.

Rogers offered a motion that a $15,000 cash dividend be paid to the owners on record as of September 10. The motion was seconded by Verga, with discussion following. Rogers explained that the dividend was less than the previous year but that the company needed to maintain a strong liquidity position to ensure growth. This motion passed unanimously.

Rogers indicated that the seventh Lakeside store would be opening on or about December 1 to take advantage of the Christmas rush. The store is being built in Williamsburg, Virginia by Rogers Development Company, a company wholly owned by Rogers and his wife. Rogers offered a motion that Lakeside sign a one-year lease for this property beginning on December 1, 2012, at a price of $21,000 per year to be paid in advance. Verga seconded this motion and discussion followed. Reese asked for an explanation for having Rogers construct the facility instead of Lakeside. The president indicated that this arrangement was designed to protect the debt/equity ratio of the company. This motion passed unanimously.

Rogers offered a motion that $200,000 be borrowed to build an addition to the company warehouse as well as to renovate the present facility. The motion was seconded by Arnold, and considerable discussion followed. Rogers stated that the warehouse roof needed immediate repair because leaks were endangering the inventory. At the same time, because of the increased growth of distributorship sales, the facility no longer would hold an adequate supply of merchandise. Rogers said that he had already received an estimate of $220,000 for both fixing the roof and increasing the size of the warehouse by approximately one-half.

Of this amount, Lakeside would borrow $200,000 and put up the rest from current funds. Concern was expressed because of the high interest rates being charged at the present time. Reese suggested that Rogers talk with several lenders in order to obtain the lowest possible rate. This motion passed unanimously. Meeting adjourned at 2:40 P.M.

Steve Reese, Secretary

Exhibit 9-2

STANDARD FORM TO CONFIRM ACCOUNT
BALANCE INFORMATION WITH FINANCIAL INSTITUTIONS

Lakeside Company
CUSTOMER NAME

Financial Institution's   [   ]
Name and Address

Lakeside Company
Box 887
Richmond, VA 23173

[

We have provided to our accountants the following information as of the close of business on **December 31, 2012**, regarding our deposit and loan balances. Please confirm the accuracy of the information noting any exceptions to the information provided. If the balances have been left blank, please complete this form by furnishing the balance in the appropriate space below. Although we do not request nor expect you to conduct a comprehensive, detailed search of your records, if, during the process of completing this confirmation, additional information about other deposit and loan accounts we may have with you comes to your attention, please include such information below. Please use the enclosed envelope to return the form directly to our accountants.

1.   At the close of business on the date listed above, our records indicated the following deposit balance(s):

ACCOUNT NAME	ACCOUNT NUMBER	INTEREST RATE	BALANCE
None			

2.   We were directly liable to the financial institution for loans at the close of business on the date listed above as follows:

ACCOUNT NO./ DESCRIPTION	BALANCE	DATE DUE	INTEREST RATE	DATE THROUGH WHICH INTEREST IS PAID	DESCRIPTION OF COLLATERAL
43731	$100,000	12/31/08	10%	NA	Lien on warehouse

Brendean Davis, Treasurer   *January 3, 2013*
(Customer's Authorized Signature)   (Date)

The information presented above by the customer is in agreement with our records. Although we have not conducted a comprehensive, detailed search of our records, no other deposit or loan accounts have come to our attention except as noted below.

Elaine Wilson   January 6, 2013
(Financial Institution Authorized Signature)   (Date)

Customer Service

EXCEPTIONS AND/OR COMMENTS
None

Please return this form directly to our accountants:

Abernethy and Chapman, CPAs
James Center - Suite 1430
Richmond, VA 23219

Ordinarily, balances are intentionally left blank if they are not available at the time the form is prepared.

Approved 1990 by American Bankers Association American Institute of Certified Public Accountants and Bank Administration Institute. Additional forms available from: AICPA-Order Department, PO Box 1003, NY, NY 10108-1003

Exhibit 9-3

RENTAL AGREEMENT

The following shall constitute a legal agreement between Rogers Development Company ("Lessor") and the Lakeside Company ("Lessee") as to the leasing of land and building ("Property") located at 910 Second Street in Williamsburg, Virginia.

The agreements between the Lessor and the Lessee are as follows:

(1)   The lease shall run from December 1, 2012, through November 30, 2013.

(2)   The Lessee shall deliver to the Lessor a payment of $21,000 prior to the initial lease date as stated above. This payment shall give the Lessee sole privilege to use the Property for the period of time of the lease.

(3)   All utilities, property taxes, and maintenance costs associated with the Property for the period of the lease shall be the sole responsibility of the Lessee.

(4)   Any permanent improvements of the property shall be the sole responsibility of the Lessee subject to prior written approval of the Lessor. Any attachments to the Property shall become the property of the Lessor subject to the laws of the Commonwealth of Virginia.

(5)   The Lessee makes no guarantee as to the value of the Property at the end of the lease period but does guarantee to repair any physical damage to the Property.

(6)   The Lessor agrees to maintain adequate insurance coverage on the Property while the Lessee agrees to maintain adequate insurance coverage on the contents therein.

LESSOR: LESSEE:
ROGERS DEVELOPMENT COMPANY   LAKESIDE COMPANY

BY: _____   BY:_____

DATE: _____   DATE: _____

Exhibit 9-4
LAKESIDE COMPANY
A/C 640-1, REPAIRS AND MAINTENANCE
12/31/2012

Invoice No.	Vendor	Invoice Date	Dollar Amount	Audit Procedures	Comments	
2891	Barnes Lumber Company	2/8/12	912.32	✓ + @	Repaired loading dock at Store 3	
2932	Jackson Tile	3/19/12	882.19	✓ + @	Renovated rest rooms at office	A
2978	Gainer Electrical	5/1/12	3142.91	✓ B + @	Rewiring of electrical system in Store 6; storm damage	
2989	Jones Ford	5/9/12	1606.93	✓ + @	Repaired company truck; accident damage	
3011	Davis Paving	6/1/12	8086.00	✓ + @	Paving and landscaping around Store 6	C
3030	Jones Ford	6/18/12	810.69	✓ + @	Repair of 3 trucks	
3052	Ridemond Paint Co.	7/5/12	1200.00	✓ + @	Repaint company offices	
3069	DZ Advertising	7/11/12	11500.00	✓ + @	Advertising for May and June	D
3106	Haymes Roofing	9/1/12	1180.00	✓ + @	Roof repairs for warehouse	
3125	Southside Shopping Center	9/20/12	15647.25	✓ + @	Renovation of Store 2	E
3144	Davis Paving	10/6/12	312.34	✓ + @	Repair warehouse parking lot	
3192	Freeman Office Equipment	11/10/12	898.00	✓ + @	Overhaul office equipment	
3209	Haymes Roofing	12/2/12	612.00	✓ + @	Roof repair for warehouse	
2950	Seymour Trash Collection	4/9/12	175.00	✓ + @	Haul away debris from warehouse repair	
3081	Ridemond Cleaning Services	7/30/12	245.00	✓ + @	Cleaning for Stores 2, 3, and 4	
3099	Jones Ford	8/6/12	62.35	✓ + @	Tune-up of company truck	
3159	Seymour Trash Collection	10/20/12	175.00	✓ + @	Trash collection	
*Various	87 other payments < $500	Various	5419.62	✓ + @	*	
	Total per General Ledger	12/31/12	53367.60	GL		
	Proposed Adjustment C		(8086.00)			
	Proposed Adjustment D		(11500.00)			
	Adjusted Total		33781.60			

Exhibit 9-5

Exhibit 9-4 (Continued)

Audit Objectives:
To verify that expenditures are legitimate and that repair and maintenance costs, properly classified, and that no portion should be capitalized.

Scope:
- Population: All changes to Repairs and Maintenance A/C 640-1.
- Sample: Judgmental—All expenditures over $500 and 10% of three less than $500, picked at random.

Audit Procedures:
✓ Traced to purchase invoice. Noted agreement as to amount and date, except B.
+ Examined purchase invoice for proper authorization.
@ Verified mathematical accuracy of invoice.
GL Traced to General Ledger noting agreement.
^ Verified footing of ledger account.

Audit Conclusion:
The account appears fairly stated in accordance with GAAP, after adjustments C, D, and pending E.

Comments
A Discussed work with Edward Thomas—appears to be legitimate expense.
B Invoice was for $3,600. Lakeside appealed bill and it was reduced by Gaines Electrical Co. Examined correspondence. Appears legitimate.
C Paving and landscaping should be capitalized.
   Proposed Adjustment:
   Land Improvements   8086-
      Repairs and Maintenance   8086-
D Apparent coding error. Advertising expense in A/C 600-1.
   Proposed Adjustment:
   Advertising Expense   11500-
      Repairs and Maintenance   11500-
E From discussions with Carol Howell, this appears to be a major renovation of Store 2. Some portion should be charged to "Leasehold Improvements." Further investigation is needed to determine amounts.

*Authors' Note: In practice, the details of these payments would be given. We have consolidated them because of space limitations.

113

Exhibit 9-5

Lakeside Company
General Ledger-Account Number 111-1
Building -Warehouse/Office

REFERENCE	DEBIT	CREDIT	BALANCE
Balance January 1, 2012			$ 248,400
Invoices # 20-34	21,800		270,200
Invoices # 1211-5	16,900		287,100
Invoice # 76679	25,300		312,400
Invoice # 1412	14,600		327,000
Total	78,600		
Balance December 31, 2012			$ 327,000

Exhibit 9-6

Invoices

Livingstone Grading and Contracting Box 911 Staples Mill Road Richmond, VA 23220 To: Lakeside Company Box 887 Richmond, VA 23173 October 5, 2012	HEILMAN CONSTRUCTION 8737 Patterson Ave. Richmond, VA 23229 Telephone: 272-4491 All Work in Done on Net 30 Terms
For Services Rendered: Grading of Land and Pouring of Foundation for New Warehouse Total Amount Due $21,800.00 This Bill is Due Immediately	Contract For: The Lakeside Company Box 887 Richmond, VA 23173 First Installment on Construction of New Warehouse This Installment Represents Work for the Month of October 2012. Amount Due - $16,900.00

Lakeside Company
Date Received: 10/7/12
Invoice # 3145
Check # 2481
Debit III-I
Approval Rogers

Lakeside Company
Date Received: 11/6/12
Invoice # 3189
Check # 2541
Debit III-I
Approval Rogers

Exhibit 9-6 (continued)

HEILMAN CONSTRUCTION
8737 Patterson Ave.
Richmond, VA 23229
Telephone: 272-4491

All Work is Done on Net 30 Terms

Contract For: The Lakeside Company
Box 887
Richmond, VA 23173

Second Installment on Construction of New Warehouse.

This Installment Represents Work for Month of November 2012.

Amount Due - $25,300.00

Lakeside Company
Date Received: 12/9/12
Invoice # 3214
Check # 2622
Debit   III-I
Approval Rogers

"Roofing Repairs and Construction"
Haynes
Roofing
11619 Huguenot Road
Richmond, VA 23234
Phone: 285-6295 or 274-6119

Lakeside Company
Box 887
Richmond, VA 23173

Roofing Repair and Construction on New Warehouse

Repair $ 3,500
New Addition   11,100
Total Bill $ 14,600

Work Performed 11/15/12 thru 12/10/12

Lakeside Company
Date Received: 12/23/12
Invoice # 3228
Check # 2668
Debit   III-I
Approval Rogers

Exhibit 9-7

HEILMAN CONSTRUCTION	Gaines Electrical Company
8737 Patterson Ave.	*"Serving Richmond since 1957"*
Richmond, VA 23229	
Telephone: 272-4491	Richmond, Virginia

HEILMAN CONSTRUCTION
8737 Patterson Ave.
Richmond, VA 23229
Telephone: 272-4491

All Work is Done on Net 30 Terms

Contract For: The Lakeside Company
Box 887
Richmond, VA 23173

Third Installment on Construction of New Warehouse.

This Installment Represents Work for Month of December 2012.

Amount Due - $17,100.00

(Gaines Electrical Company)
"Serving Richmond since 1957"

Richmond, Virginia

Lakeside Company
Box 887
Richmond, VA 23173

Electrical service on new construction for two weeks - 12/28/12 - 1/8/13

$4,800.00

Terms: Net 30

Mail Check to: Gaines Electrical Company
Box 9166, Broad Street
Richmond, VA 23219

Lakeside Company
Date Received: 1/7/13
Invoice # 3316
Check # 2780
Debit   III-I
Approval Rogers

Lakeside Company
Date Received: 1/15/13
Invoice # 3408
Check # 2881
Debit   III-I
Approval Rogers

The Lakeside Company: Auditing Cases

10. SAMPLING FOR ATTRIBUTES

On February 4, 2013, Jan Luck, assistant controller for the Lakeside Company, delivered to the Abernethy and Chapman auditors an analysis of all vendor invoices received by the company during December and January. A total of 283 invoices had been located by Luck with assistance from the independent auditors. These bills represented a variety of charges incurred by each of the company's stores including rent, heating oil, electricity, insurance, water, maintenance fees, property taxes, and advertising. In addition, a number of the invoices reflected the travel and lodging expenses of the members of Lakeside's sales staff.

For each of these invoices, Luck had scheduled the total amount owed by Lakeside, the expense or asset account to be charged, the due date, and the date paid or the date on which payment would be made. Luck also calculated and listed the portion of each bill that was legally owed by Lakeside as of December 31, 2012. Based on this analysis, accrued expenses totaling $46,311 were to be recorded by the company as a year-end adjusting entry.

Carole Mitchell, senior auditor with the Abernethy and Chapman organization, was aware that she would have to verify the accuracy of the $46,311 accrual. As with all client-prepared computations, the auditing firm had a responsibility to establish the validity of this liability. In this instance, though, the need to review the analysis was especially important since a large change was being made in the net income figure reported by the client.

Mitchell was primarily interested in Luck's ability to allocate these expenses correctly between 2012 and 2013. In arriving at the $46,311 accrual, every invoice had been examined by Luck in order to assign the appropriate amount to each period. Because of the potential audit time involved, Mitchell wanted to avoid having to assign a member of her staff to review and check all 283 documents. Instead, she hoped to validate the client's work by analyzing a representative sample of these invoices. Mitchell knows that there are two major types of sampling methods: sampling for attributes and sampling for variables. With sampling for attributes, the auditor is concerned with the rate of occurrence of a particular characteristic, such as the error rate in connection with the application of a control procedure being in place or not. With sampling for variables, the auditor is concerned with estimating a balance, such as the appropriate dollar value of an account or a transaction.

Since Mitchell was concerned with the occurrence of errors in the allocation process, she decided to apply sampling for attributes.[1] Based on Mitchell's previous work with sampling for attributes on other audit clients, she realized that she had to establish three parameters corresponding to her judgment of the client and the importance of the procedure being evaluated:

Acceptable Risk of Assessing Control Risk Too Low (ARACR). Because of the decision to sample, Mitchell understood that a degree of risk was involved. Since all of the invoices were not to be reviewed, a possibility existed that the auditing firm would evaluate Luck's work as being reliable when, in fact, it was not. After some consideration, Mitchell chose a 10% ARACR for this test. She was willing to accept the statistical fact that one time in ten the sample would mislead her into relying on work that was not actually acceptable.

Estimated Population Exception Rate (EPER). Based on the degree of complexity involved in the allocation process, Mitchell realized that Luck would probably commit some errors; perfection was not anticipated for this type of task. In a statistical sampling plan designed to determine the frequency of an attribute, the auditor must estimate an actual occurrence rate. From discussions with Luck as well as observations of her work, Mitchell believed that a 3% exception rate should be considered normal.

Tolerable Exception Rate (TER). Finally, Mitchell had to address the possibility that the errors existing in the population were of a quantity significant enough to nullify reliance on Luck's work. Mitchell decided that if a sample indicated the presence of an error rate in excess of 6% she would be forced to devise alternative procedures to verify the end-of-year accrual.

Mitchell's next concern was the determination of the number of invoices that had to be selected to furnish the desired level of assurance. Because of the frequent use of sampling for attributes, the CPA firm of Abernethy and Chapman provides its auditors with statistical tables to assist them in the implementation of this testing procedure. Based on predetermined mathematical calculations, the proper size for any sample can be found on these tables. The specific table to be used is determined by the auditor's decision concerning the ARACR. Exhibit 10-1 presents the table for a 10% ARACR, the level chosen by Mitchell for this test. The appropriate sample size is a function of the EPER (left column) and the chosen TER (top row).

After Mitchell selects the sample and analyzes individual items, conclusions about the population as a whole will be derived by using a second table. Exhibit 10-2 presents mathematical results based on the auditor's desire to limit the ARACR to 10%. The sample size (left column) and the actual number of exceptions discovered in the sample (top row)

---

[1]In Case 11, Mitchell tests the appropriate dollar amount of the liability using sampling for variables.

provide the computed upper exception rate (CUER) anticipated in the population. However, this upper exception rate is not intended as a precise indication of the percentage of mistakes that are present. Rather, Mitchell can assume, given the three parameters that she has set, that the exception rate in the 283 allocations is no higher than the percentage indicated in Exhibit 10-2. Consequently, if the computed upper exception rate is equal to or less than the 6% tolerable exception rate established as a prerequisite, the number of errors in Luck's work will be judged as acceptable. Mitchell will still have to analyze the individual errors found in the sample since both the type as well as quantity of mistakes must be evaluated.

Prior to the start of this testing, Mitchell makes one final calculation. The table produced in Exhibit 10-1 is based on a large population and a sampling plan with replacement where items chosen will be recorded and then returned to the population. Lakeside has only 283 invoices, and the auditors will not replace selected items to avoid having them chosen a second time. Mitchell is aware that a finite correction factor can be applied to adjust the information found in this table so that it corresponds with the client's population. In some cases, this adjustment significantly reduces the required number of items to be tested, thus, increasing audit efficiency. The formula applied for this purpose is

$$\text{Appropriate Sample Size} \quad = \quad \frac{n'}{1 + \left(\dfrac{n'}{N} \right)}$$

where: n' = sample size found in table
N = number of items in the population.

DISCUSSION QUESTIONS

(1) Independent auditors must evaluate an entire set of financial statements. Considering that risk is always involved in selecting only a sample, why are auditors willing to accept less than a complete review and analysis when accumulating evidence?

(2) Incorporating statistics into a sampling plan creates additional complexity for the auditor. What are the advantages of sampling plans that are based on statistical laws and guidelines?

(3) Sampling for attributes is a procedure that is frequently associated in auditing with the tests of controls. Why is this type of statistical sampling especially important in evaluating the degree to which a client's internal control procedures are effective?

(4) When applying sampling for attributes, auditors often attempt to measure several attributes within a single testing plan. What is the reason for this approach? What other attribute could be tested by Mitchell in this case?

(5)   Mitchell has indicated that she assumes Luck has made some mistakes in allocating year-end expenses. How can the auditor tolerate using work that is known to be incorrect? Why might an individual such as Luck commit errors in arriving at a year-end adjustment?

(6)   Mitchell anticipates that Luck has committed errors in 3% (EPER) of the allocations made. How does an auditor arrive at this type of estimation?

(7)   Mitchell has decided that Luck's work will be viewed as being reliable if the sample indicates 6% (TER) or fewer errors. What factors should have influenced the auditor's selection of this parameter?

(8)   Assume that Mitchell's computations indicate an appropriate sample size of 40. She selects this number of invoices and reviews the accuracy of Luck's allocations. Mitchell discovers two errors. What conclusion will she reach based on the parameters established?

(9)   Assume that Mitchell selects a sample of 40 items and determines from these allocations that Luck's work is not reliable. What alternatives are available to the auditor?

EXERCISE

(1)   To ensure adequate documentation, the CPA firm of Abernethy and Chapman requires its auditors to complete a preprinted form whenever sampling for attributes is being applied. This document is presented in Exhibit 10-3. [Case10-1.doc]

a) Complete the form using the data provided in this case. Assume that a sample of the appropriate size is drawn by Mitchell using a random number generator on her computer. Also, assume that Mitchell discovers two errors in the sample, although both are of relatively small amounts and appear to be caused by errors of addition.

b) How would your answer in a) change if three errors were discovered instead of two?

APPLY YOUR RESEARCH

Use library resources such as searchable databases to research the following topic.

(1)   Write a report discussing the use of sampling in conducting an audit. To what extent should auditors use sampling? Is statistical sampling better than non-statistical sampling? What problems do auditors face when using sampling methods?

121

CONSULTING PARTNER REVIEW

Bob Zimmerman, the consulting partner on the Lakeside engagement, is concerned about the following issues and would like for you to respond to them. The audio clips are available online at www.prenhall.com/arens.

(1)   Eliminating all risk

(2)   Creating changes in sample size

Exhibit 10-1

DETERMINING SAMPLE SIZE FOR ATTRIBUTES SAMPLING
10 Percent ARACR

EPER**	Tolerable Exception Rate (%)										
(%)	2	3	4	5	6	7	8	9	10	15	20
0.00	114	76	57	45	38	32	28	25	22	15	11
0.25	194	129	96	77	64	55	48	42	38	25	18
0.50	194	129	96	77	64	55	48	42	38	25	18
1.00	*	176	96	77	64	55	48	42	38	25	18
1.25	*	221	132	77	64	55	48	42	38	25	18
1.50	*	*	132	105	64	55	48	42	38	25	18
2.00	*	*	198	132	88	75	48	42	38	25	18
2.25	*	*	*	132	88	75	65	42	38	25	18
2.50	*	*	*	158	110	75	65	58	38	25	18
3.00	*	*	*	*	132	94	65	58	52	25	18
3.25	*	*	*	*	153	113	82	58	52	25	18
3.50	*	*	*	*	194	113	82	73	52	25	18
4.00	*	*	*	*	*	149	98	73	65	25	18
4.50	*	*	*	*	*	218	130	87	65	34	18
5.00	*	*	*	*	*	*	160	115	78	34	18
5.50	*	*	*	*	*	*	*	142	103	34	18

*Sample is too large to be cost effective for most audit applications.

**Expected Population Exception Rate (EPER)

Exhibit 10-2

EVALUATING SAMPLE RESULTS USING
ATTRIBUTES SAMPLING
10 Percent ARACR

Sample Size	Actual Number of Exceptions Found										
	0	**1**	**2**	**3**	**4**	**5**	**6**	**7**	**8**	**9**	**10**
20	10.9	18.1	*	*	*	*	*	*	*	*	*
25	8.8	14.7	19.9	*	*	*	*	*	*	*	*
30	7.4	12.4	16.8	*	*	*	*	*	*	*	*
35	6.4	10.7	14.5	18.1	*	*	*	*	*	*	*
40	5.6	9.4	12.8	15.9	19.0	*	*	*	*	*	*
45	5.0	8.4	11.4	14.2	17.0	19.6	*	*	*	*	*
50	4.5	7.6	10.3	12.9	15.4	17.8	*	*	*	*	*
55	4.1	6.9	9.4	11.7	14.0	16.2	18.4	*	*	*	*
60	3.8	6.3	8.6	10.8	12.9	14.9	16.9	18.8	*	*	*
70	3.2	5.4	7.4	9.3	11.1	12.8	14.6	16.2	17.9	19.5	*
80	2.8	4.8	6.5	8.3	9.7	11.3	12.8	14.3	15.7	17.2	18.6
90	2.5	4.3	5.8	7.3	8.7	10.1	11.4	12.7	14.0	15.3	16.6
100	2.3	3.8	5.2	6.6	7.8	9.1	10.3	11.5	12.7	13.8	15.0
120	1.9	3.2	4.4	5.5	6.6	7.6	8.6	9.6	10.6	11.6	12.5
160	1.4	2.4	3.3	4.1	4.9	5.7	6.5	7.2	8.0	8.7	9.5
200	1.1	1.9	2.6	3.3	4.0	4.6	5.2	5.8	6.4	7.0	7.6

* Over 20 percent

Exhibit 10-3

Abernethy and Chapman

SAMPLING FOR ATTRIBUTES

Client:

Year Ending:

Audit Area:

Date of Testing:

(1)   State the objectives of the audit testing:

(2)   Define the attribute or attributes to be estimated:

(3)   Define the population:

(4)   Define the sampling unit:

(5)   Specify the acceptable risk of assessing control risk too low, and discuss any factors affecting this decision:

(6)   Estimate the exception rate of the population, and discuss any factors affecting this estimation:

125

(7)   Specify the tolerable exception rate, and discuss any factors affecting this decision:

(8)   Indicate the sample size, and show the use of the finite correction factor if applicable:

(9)   Indicate the method used to draw a random sample:

(10)   Indicate the number of exceptions discovered, the rate of exceptions in the sample, and the computed upper exception rate in the population:

(11)   From a quantitative perspective, is the population reliable? (Include the rationale for your answer):

(12)   Describe the types of exceptions that were found:

(13)   Recommendations:

The Lakeside Company: Auditing Cases

11. SAMPLING FOR VARIABLES - DIFFERENCE ESTIMATION

Note: The material presented herein is based on the problem introduced in Case 10. Once again, the auditor is attempting to obtain assurance as to the validity of the client's representation. However, in this current case, an alternative approach is being examined. Although the previous case should serve as background information, the assumption is made here in Case 11 that a sampling for attributes plan has <u>not</u> been applied.

During the later stages of every Abernethy and Chapman engagement, the partner in charge performs a comprehensive review of all audit documentation created by the audit team. Although each of these documents is examined for completeness, clarity, and understandability, the primary purpose of this procedure is to ensure that sufficient, competent evidence has been accumulated to substantiate the audit opinion. To stress the importance of this responsibility, the firm requires the partner to "sign-off" on each major audit area to indicate the belief that reasonable assurance has been achieved and that no material misstatements exist within the client's financial statements.

Dan Cline is the partner in charge of the 2012 audit of the Lakeside Company. During his final review on every engagement, Cline creates a list of issues that he believes need to be clarified or resolved before the audit is concluded. One of the areas that Cline has noted in the Lakeside examination is the cut-off testing performed on the client's year-end expense accrual. An adjustment to record a $46,311 liability was proposed by Lakeside and tentatively accepted by Carole Mitchell, the audit senior. According to her audit documentation, Mitchell analyzed 30 out of 283 invoices prior to recommending that this accrual be accepted. Cline was concerned to note that the liability computed on 4 of these 30 invoices contained errors committed by Lakeside personnel. Only 10.6% (=30/283) of the invoices had been reviewed by Mitchell and those documents reflected a 13.3% (=4/30) error rate. Cline was not satisfied that sufficient corroborating evidence had been obtained to substantiate the $46,311 accrual.

In a subsequent discussion to finalize any remaining audit actions, Mitchell and Cline assessed the need for additional evidence to validate the client's expense accrual:

MITCHELL: I judgmentally chose a sample size of 30 invoices. I believed then, as I do now, that I could arrive at a proper conclusion about the total accrual by examining approximately 10% of the invoices. Mistakes were found, which I have documented, but they involved relatively small amounts and did not show any suspicious trends. I recognize that $46,311 is not a precisely correct amount, but I still believe that this accrual is a fairly presented figure. I see no reason to waste further audit time.

CLINE: I don't necessarily disagree that Lakeside's balance is fairly presented; I just don't believe we have proven that assertion in our audit documentation. If the entire population contains 13.3% errors, approximately 38 of the 283 (=13.3% × 283) accruals are incorrect. That represents a lot of mistakes, and we have not computed a possible total dollar amount for these errors. Even small errors can add up to a large deviation if enough are present. Furthermore, the population may actually hold more than 13.3% errors. Our single sample of only 30 invoices might not have been representative.

MITCHELL: In that case, I see no alternative but to examine more of the invoices.

CLINE: That approach would indeed provide us with a better estimation of the error rate. However, we already know the population has errors. I am more interested in the dollar impact of those mistakes. Do they net to zero or $20,000 or perhaps even more?

MITCHELL: We can always recompute an accrual for each of the invoices. The total amount of the liability could be determined to the penny in that way.

CLINE: Examining the entire population would take too long and we really have no need for that degree of accuracy. I will be satisfied if we can verify that Lakeside's $46,311 figure is within $8,000 of the real total. Could we use some form of sampling for variables plan and estimate the total dollar amount of these errors?

MITCHELL: I suppose so but I have had little experience in applying sampling for variables concepts.

CLINE: Why don't you talk with Mike Farrell? He is our partner specializing in statistical sampling. I am certain that he can assist you in designing a statistical sampling plan to determine the validity of the client's accrual. After you complete the testing, let's review the results to see if we have the assurance that we need.

Mitchell did approach Farrell with her problem, and he provided the following information:

"Several types of statistical sampling approaches exist but each is based on selecting a representative sample. A truly representative sample has the same characteristics as the population. Thus, evaluations and decisions can be made about the population just by looking at the sample. To achieve a reasonable degree of representation, two conditions must be met. First, a large enough sample is selected, and second, all items are chosen randomly. Mathematical equations are used to project the

128

appropriate sample size while our firm generates random numbers with a computer program.

"Sampling for variables is a technique used specifically for calculating a total which, in this case, is the client's expense accrual. After you have defined the population and the sampling unit, an estimate is made of the standard deviation of the individual units within the population. *Standard deviation* is a statistical measure of the dispersion of items from their arithmetic mean. Are the individual numbers close together or far apart? This figure is important since a larger dispersion necessitates a larger sample being drawn. Auditors derive an estimation of the standard deviation by a mathematical formula. Several variations of this equation exist but at Abernethy and Chapman the following model is used:

Estimated Standard Deviation $= \sqrt{\dfrac{\sum (e)^2 - n(\bar{e})^2}{n-1}}$

"In this formula, e is the value of each unit sampled while $\bar{e}$ is the average of these items. The letter n represents the number of items selected. Although we usually need to choose between 30 and 50 items for this computation, five can be used here for demonstration purposes. Assume that the five numbers selected had values of $1, $5, $5, $7, and $12.

e	e^2
1	1
5	25
5	25
7	49
12	144
Σ 30	244

$\bar{e} = 30 \div 5$ or $\underline{6}$

"With this small sample, the standard deviation would be:

$$\sqrt{\frac{244 - (5)(6)^2}{5-1}} = \sqrt{\frac{244 - 180}{4}} = 4$$

"Once the standard deviation has been estimated, the auditor must establish the maximum level of risk that can be tolerated. In sampling for variables, two separate risks are encountered. First, an acceptable risk of incorrect acceptance, referred to as ARIA, has to be set. This percentage represents the possibility that Abernethy and Chapman will accept the client's $46,311 accrual even though, in actuality, the figure is materially in error. Setting a risk level for incorrect acceptance is a serious responsibility since it establishes the possibility that the auditor could render an unqualified opinion on statements that are not fairly presented. Fortunately, an effective control structure as well as any other substantive procedures the auditor is performing in the area can lessen the risk of incorrect acceptance.

"Auditors also have to set an acceptable level for the risk of incorrect rejection, commonly known as ARIR. In the Lakeside case, our firm faces the possibility of rejecting the $46,311 accrual based on a sample when the figure may in fact be fairly presented. Incorrect rejection usually causes the auditor to perform extra substantive tests that are not necessary. This causes inefficiencies. As a worse possibility, the firm might qualify financial statements that are actually fairly presented.

"Through the use of sampling for variables, the auditor is able to compute the correct sample size based on predetermined limits as to the risks being taken. An acceptable risk of incorrect acceptance is required as well as an acceptable risk of incorrect rejection. Both of these figures are ultimately derived from the auditor's judgment. Unfortunately, the two risk levels cannot be entered directly into the various statistical equations. Instead, equivalent confidence coefficients, sometimes referred to as Z values, are utilized for mathematical purposes. These equivalents can be found from a statistical table (see Exhibit 11-1).

"After estimating the standard deviation and setting the two acceptable risk levels, the next preliminary task is to establish a *tolerable misstatement*, the amount of mistake that the auditor is willing to accept in the client's reported balance. From your discussion with Dan Cline, tolerable misstatement will be $8,000 in this audit test of the accrual balance.

"Before proceeding to the statistical formulas, a decision is needed as to the specific type of sampling for variables plan to be applied. For example, one common approach is referred to as mean-per-unit sampling. Using this method, the arithmetic average of the sample is assumed to be the same as that of the population. As an illustration, if the average end-of-year accrual found in a Lakeside sample came to $165, that figure would be multiplied by the 283 invoices to arrive at an estimated total. Unfortunately, one major problem often hinders the usefulness of the mean-per-unit approach. The standard deviation of most populations is usually so high that a very large sample is necessary; thus, the principal benefit of sampling, saving time, is defeated.

"I would suggest that you consider using an alternative known as *difference estimation*. It is appropriate when individual book values can be compared with audited balances to arrive at a population of differences. This statistical sampling technique estimates the total of the differences rather than the total of the audited values. For Lakeside, the year-end expense accrual would not be calculated directly, but rather its distance from $46,311.

Since the individual differences in most populations tend to be zero or small numbers, the standard deviation of these differences will be relatively low. Thus, a smaller sample is required to achieve the auditor's acceptable risk levels. The Lakeside situation lends itself to this procedure since the client already has an accrual for each invoice that can now be measured against an audited value.

"To begin using difference estimation, I would utilize the 30 items that have already been randomly selected (Exhibit 11-2) to compute an advance estimation of the standard deviation. The formula previously discussed should be used for this purpose. *Remember though that the items being sampled are the differences.* For example, if the client reports an accrual of $140 but our analysis indicates an actual expense of $145, an understatement of $5 exists. This $5 figure is a unit within our population and will be used in calculating the standard deviation and then the total difference that the actual accrual is from $46,311. That is, use the "difference" column in Exhibit 12-2 to compute the standard deviation.

"After the standard deviation of the differences is estimated, the appropriate sample size can be calculated using the following formula:

$$\text{Sample Size} = \left[\frac{SD \times (Z_a + Z_r) \times N}{TM - E} \right]^2$$

where:

N	=	population size
Z_a	=	confidence coefficient for the acceptable risk of incorrect acceptance (Exhibit 11-1)
Z_r	=	confidence coefficient for the acceptable risk of incorrect rejection (Exhibit 11-1)
SD	=	estimate of the standard deviation of the *differences*
TM	=	tolerable misstatement of the population
E	=	point estimate of population misstatement

"We have discussed all of the elements of this equation except for *E*, the point estimate of the population misstatement. By looking at last year's audit or by examining the quality of the client's work, the total dollar misstatement existing within the population can be anticipated. Since our firm did not audit Lakeside last year, you may want to use the average misstatement in the initial sample of 30 invoices as the estimation of this figure.

"Once the sample size has been determined, the appropriate number of invoices should be selected randomly and examined. Any difference between the client accrual and the audited balance is listed. To save time, most auditors would include within their sample the 30 items previously analyzed in determining the standard deviation. The average difference for the entire sample is then computed with that amount being considered a reflection of the population of 283 items. For example, if the average difference of the sample proved to be +$10, we would estimate that the accrual actually exceeded $46,311 by $2,830 (+$10 multiplied by the 283 invoices).

"This $2,830 figure, however, is just a single point. Since only a portion of the population was examined, this degree of absolute accuracy is not possible. Hence, the auditor computes a range, a *precision interval*, that serves as the actual estimate of the population total. In deriving this precision interval, the auditor must first reestimate the standard deviation since a larger sample is now available. The standard deviation formula previously discussed is again used for this purpose with the refined figure helping to ensure the accuracy of the final evaluation.

"The precision interval can then be calculated using another mathematical equation:

Precision Interval = $N \times Z_a \times \dfrac{SD}{\sqrt{n}} \times \sqrt{\dfrac{N-n}{N}}$

where:

N	=	population size
n	=	total sample size
SD	=	estimate of standard deviation (second computation)
Z_a	=	confidence coefficient for the acceptable risk of incorrect acceptance (Exhibit 11-1)

"To illustrate, assume that the point estimation of the errors is calculated as being $2,830 above book value. According to the sample, the client's total appears to be understated by that amount. Assume also that a precision interval of $5,000 is computed using the above equation. Given the risk parameters that have been established by the auditor, the actual error apparently lies somewhere between an understatement of $7,830 ($2,830 + $5,000) and an overstatement of $2,170 ($2,830 - $5,000). Because sampling has been used, the exact population total cannot be specified within that range. However, since Cline wants assurance that the client figure is within $8,000 of the real total, the auditing firm can accept the $46,311 as fairly presented. No portion of the computed range falls outside of that $8,000 boundary; the risk is acceptable. Conversely, if the sample had indicated a range from an overstatement of $1,000 to an understatement of $9,000, the client's accrual could not be accepted without further testing; the interval achieved would not be completely within the $8,000 tolerable risk level. The $46,311 reported balance might still be fairly presented but too much risk would be involved in accepting the figure without gathering additional audit evidence."

After talking with Farrell, Carole Mitchell met again briefly with Cline to establish guidelines for this testing. The decision was made that a tolerable error of $8,000 should be used. In addition, an acceptable risk of incorrect acceptance of 10% was set along with a 30% level for the risk of incorrect rejection.

DISCUSSION QUESTIONS

(1) Carole Mitchell attempted to use judgmental sampling to verify the client's accrual in this case while Dan Cline opted for statistical sampling. What are the advantages and disadvantages of each approach? Will a statistical sample usually be smaller than a nonstatistical sample?

(2) Exhibit 11-2 presents the results of Mitchell's initial testing. Was Cline correct in seeking additional audit evidence? Include in your answer the concept of sufficiency of audit evidence.

(3) Statistical sampling is occasionally criticized for preventing the auditor from introducing personal judgment into a particular test. Is this assertion valid? How much knowledge of statistical sampling should the auditor have? Is it typical to obtain assistance from a specialist in developing a sample?

(4) Statistical sampling has also been criticized for being a slow, time-consuming process relative to judgmental sampling. Is this assertion valid?

(5) An auditor may utilize sampling for attributes in some tests and sampling for variables in others. How is the decision made as to which of these methods should be applied? Is it appropriate to use a cost-based decision when considering the independent auditors' responsibility?

(6) Assume that Mitchell conducts her sampling plan and calculates the estimation of the total deviations to be +$3,760 with a precision interval of $5,200. What will be her conclusion about the population and what actions should be taken next by the auditors?

EXERCISE

(1) To ensure adequate documentation, the CPA firm of Abernethy and Chapman requires its auditors to complete preprinted forms whenever sampling for variables is being applied. [Case11-1.doc]

    (a)   Exhibit 11-4 presents the document to be used in computing an initial representative sample size. Complete this form using the data provided in this case and the initial sample of 30 invoices.

    (b)   Exhibit 11-5 presents the document to be used in evaluating the results of a difference estimation sample. Independent of your answer in (a), assume that Mitchell has computed the need for a sample size of 50 invoices. Consequently, she selects the 20 additional items found in Exhibit 11-3 using a computer-generated list of random numbers. Complete the form found in Exhibit 11-5 based on the data provided in this case. Assume that the sample size is 50; thus, use both the initial sample of 30 invoices (Exhibit 11-2) *and* the additional sample of 20 invoices (Exhibit 11-3) to complete this document.

(2) Exhibit 11-5 presents the document to be used in evaluating the results of a difference estimation sample. Independent of your answer in (1a), assume that Mitchell has computed the need for a sample size of 50 invoices. Using the additional data file, draw a random sample of 50 invoices, and complete the form found in Exhibit 11-5 based on the data set provided in the additional data file. [Case 11-1.doc and Case11-1.xls]

CONSULTING PARTNER REVIEW

Bob Zimmerman, the consulting partner on the Lakeside engagement, is concerned about the following issues and would like for you to respond to them. The audio clips are available online at www.prenhall.com/arens.

(1) What if the sample does not substantiate the client figure?
(2) How does materiality affect individual accounts?

Exhibit 11-1

CONFIDENCE COEFFICIENTS
ACCEPTABLE LEVELS OF RISK

Acceptable Risk of Incorrect Acceptance (ARIA)	Acceptable Risk of Incorrect Rejection (ARIR)	Confidence Coefficient (Z Value)
2.5%	5.0%	1.96
5.0%	10.0%	1.64
10.0%	20.0%	1.28
12.5%	25.0%	1.15
15.0%	30.0%	1.04
20.0%	40.0%	0.84
25.0%	50.0%	0.67
30.0%	60.0%	0.52
40.0%	80.0%	0.25
50.0%	100.0%	0.00

Exhibit 11-2

INITIAL SAMPLE OF YEAR-END INVOICES

Invoice	Book Value	Audited Value	Audited Value Minus Book Value*
1	$1,347	$1,347	-0-
2	44	44	-0-
3	168	168	-0-
4	-0-**	-0-	-0-
5	135	340	205
6	-0-	-0-	-0-
7	802	802	-0-
8	76	76	-0-
9	126	126	-0-
10	-0-	-0-	-0-
11	269	269	-0-
12	488	488	-0-
13	561	561	-0-
14	-0-	49	49
15	102	102	-0-
16	22	22	-0-
17	410	300	(110)
18	-0-	-0-	-0-
19	176	176	-0-
20	88	88	-0-
21	400	400	-0-
22	247	247	-0-
23	120	276	156
24	55	55	-0-
25	131	131	-0-
26	1,088	1,088	-0-
27	-0-	-0-	-0-
28	-0-	-0-	-0-
29	50	50	-0-
30	632	632	-0-

*Parentheses indicate that the client's balance is overstated.

**Zero balances represent invoices received in January that were entirely for January expenses.

Exhibit 11-3

ADDITIONAL SAMPLE OF 20 INVOICES

Invoice	Book Value	Audited Value	Audited Value Less Book Value
31	$ 331	$ 331	-0-
32	-0-	-0-	-0-
33	211	211	-0-
34	75	75	-0-
35	108	108	-0-
36	549	549	-0-
37	35	35	-0-
38	297	200	$ (97)
39	380	380	-0-
40	50	50	-0-
41	-0-	-0-	-0-
42	185	185	-0-
43	400	400	-0-
44	124	124	-0-
45	250	100	(150)
46	24	24	-0-
47	-0-	47	47
48	278	278	-0-
49	-0-	-0-	-0-
50	-0-	-0-	-0-

Exhibit 11-4

Abernethy and Chapman

DETERMINATION OF INITIAL SAMPLE SIZE
SAMPLING FOR VARIABLES

Client:

Form Completed By:

Audit Area:

Date of Testing: _____ Year Ending:

(1) Estimate the standard deviation of the population. Show the formula being used and identify each element within this formula.

(2) Specify the acceptable level of risk for incorrect acceptance. Identify the confidence coefficient (Z value) for this percentage. Include any considerations that were used in arriving at this parameter.

(3) Specify the acceptable level of risk for incorrect rejection. Identify the confidence coefficient (Z value) for this percentage. Include any considerations that were used in arriving at this parameter.

(4) Specify a tolerable misstatement for this population. Include any considerations that were used in arriving at this parameter.

(5) Specify a point estimate of the population misstatement. Describe the method by which this determination was made.

(6) Calculate the appropriate initial sample size. Show the formula being used and identify each element within this formula.

Exhibit 11-5

Abernethy and Chapman

SAMPLING PLAN FOR VARIABLES -
DIFFERENCE ESTIMATION

Client:

Form Completed By:

Audit Area:

Date of Testing: _____ Year Ending:

(1) State the objectives of the audit testing and define misstatement conditions:

(2) Define the population:

(3) Define the sampling unit:

(4) Specify the acceptable level of risk for incorrect acceptance and identify the confidence coefficient (Z value) for this percentage:

(5) Specify the acceptable level of risk for incorrect rejection and identify the confidence coefficient (Z value) for this percentage:

(6) Specify a tolerable misstatement for this population:

(7) Specify a point estimate of the population misstatement [use the initial sample]:

(8) Compute appropriate sample size:

[Note: Given at 50 in this case; thus, do not compute the sample size here].

(9) Indicate the method used to draw a random sample:

(10) Recompute the standard deviation using the entire sample selected:

(11) Calculate the average difference within the entire sample and extend this figure to the entire population:

(12) Determine the precision interval. Show the formula being used and identify each element within this formula (all computations should be included):

(13) Identify the upper and lower confidence limits of the population based on the precision interval and the average difference of the sample:

(14) Indicate whether the upper and lower confidence limits lie entirely within the tolerable error parameters:

(15) Conclusion/Recommendation:

The Lakeside Company: Auditing Cases

12.   REVIEW OF SUBSEQUENT EVENTS

During the last part of January 2013, Carole Mitchell, senior auditor for the CPA firm of Abernethy and Chapman, was in the process of finishing the substantive testing for the Lakeside Company audit engagement. She hoped to complete fieldwork by February 9 in order to have the final audit report delivered to the client by the February 22 deadline.

The examination had moved into its final phases, and Mitchell, along with the other members of the audit team, were now accumulating evidence relating to the weeks subsequent to the end of the client's fiscal year. They had already performed the following testing procedures in the period since December 31, 2012:

1.   Confirmations were returned to the auditors by each of the banks that dealt with Lakeside during the year (see Exhibit 9-2). These documents disclosed year-end balances and the terms for all accounts and loans. The confirmations also requested the banks to furnish information on certain types of contingent liabilities such as discounted notes receivable. Upon receipt of each confirmation, Paul Rubens reconciled the reported balances to Lakeside's December 31, 2012 records to ensure their agreement. In addition, Carole Mitchell verified that the terms of each loan were consistent with the accounting records of the company. She also made certain that all loans were being appropriately disclosed within the financial statements.

2.   Cut-off statements were received from each bank for all of Lakeside's checking accounts. These statements covered the period from January 1, 2013, through January 10, 2013. Rubens verified that all canceled checks and deposits returned by the bank agreed with the year-end reconciliations prepared by Lakeside employees.

3.   Another Abernethy and Chapman auditor, Art Heyman, established the validity of the year-end inventory and sales cutoff. Using the bills of lading prepared between December 28, 2012, and January 2, 2013, (see Exhibit 8-3), Heyman located the corresponding sales invoices to determine the appropriate date for recognizing each sale. This information was then compared with the actual recording of the transaction in Lakeside's Sales Journal. Heyman also traced the receiving reports for the same period to the purchase invoices to ascertain the date on which title changed hands for each incoming shipment. These dates were then reconciled to the Inventory Purchases Journal to ensure that all purchases were recorded in the correct time period.

4. Wallace Andrews, the audit manager for the Lakeside engagement, read the minutes of a board of directors meeting held on January 17, 2013. The directors had met primarily to discuss two matters: the expansion of the warehouse facility and damage to Store 2 caused by an electrical fire on January 5, 2013. At this meeting, Rogers stated that the construction was progressing as expected and should be completed during March at a cost of approximately $440,000. He also reported that an electrical malfunction in Store 2 had started a small fire on the evening of January 5. Actual fire damage was limited, but water and heavy smoke had caused over $80,000 in inventory losses. Rogers indicated that the company's insurance would cover between 60% and 80% of this amount. As a final action, the board of directors declared a cash dividend of $16,000 to be paid to shareholders on January 31, 2013.

5. Carole Mitchell began to review a portion of the invoices received by Lakeside during the month of January 2013. She also intended to analyze the company's cash disbursements for this same period. Both procedures were designed to detect any liabilities that were unrecorded by the client as of December 31, 2012 (see Cases 10 and 11).

6. Mitchell performed an extensive search for contingent losses. She talked with Lakeside's management about the possible existence of such losses, read correspondence as well as invoices received from the law firm of Benzinger and Dawkins (the outside legal counsel employed by Lakeside), and reviewed all bank confirmations along with the company's current contracts. None of these procedures indicated the presence of any type of contingent loss as of December 31, 2012. A letter was then mailed to Benzinger and Dawkins stating that the management of Lakeside did not believe any material contingencies existed. On February 2, 2013, Abernethy and Chapman received a response stating that the law firm did not differ with the evaluation of contingencies made by the Lakeside management.

7. A related parties' inquiry letter was sent to the Rogers Development Company owned by Mr. and Mrs. Rogers. This letter asked about the extent and nature of dealings with Lakeside, as well as all amounts due to or from that company. Rogers' reply described the lease agreement on Store 7, but nothing more.

8. Mitchell performed a final analytical review. This review is in addition to the one done during the preliminary stages of the audit (see Case 3). The purpose of the earlier analytical review was to help identify critical or problem areas for further substantive testing. The purpose of this final analytical review is to ensure that nothing unusual has occurred during the latter stages of the audit. If unusual fluctuations occur, then the auditor must investigate further.

    One issue still concerned Mitchell. She had recently reviewed the year-end adjustment entries prepared by Lakeside. Most of these entries were routine: depreciation

142

expense, payroll liability, interest expense accrual, etc. One entry, though, did catch her attention: a debit to Other Miscellaneous Expenses and a credit to Accrued Product Warranty for $90,930. When questioned, Mark Hayes, the controller, stated that this adjusting entry was made annually to recognize the company's obligation for future repairs on products that had been sold under warranty during the past year. He indicated that the former auditors, King and Associates, had suggested some years ago that Lakeside accrue 0.7% of its annual sales as product warranty. Since that time, a similar adjusting entry had been made each year. Hayes stated that 2012 sales of $12,990,000 required an accrual of $90,930 based on the 0.7% rate.

In further discussion with Hayes, Mitchell discovered that Lakeside offers a six-month warranty on all merchandise. If any item malfunctions within that time, Lakeside will repair it at no cost to the customer. The services of several local repair shops are used for this purpose. When asked about the cost, Hayes responded, "It usually runs about $8,000 per month. The Cypress products are good; repairs are not that common."

Mitchell immediately went to Dan Cline, the audit partner on the engagement, for guidance. Estimating the potential liability of a six-month product warranty on $13 million in sales was an obvious audit concern. Cline agreed that additional evidence was needed to corroborate the accrued liability balance reported at December 31, 2012. He asked Mitchell to prepare a two-year history of repairs so that a determination could be made of the client's potential liability. Mitchell requested this data from Hayes. Hayes was able to break down the repair expense for each month by the age of the item being repaired. This information is contained in Exhibit 12-1.

DISCUSSION QUESTIONS

(1)   In examining a bank cut-off statement, what evidence is the auditor seeking?

(2)   Why do auditors continue to send confirmation letters to banks if the client's account has been closed? Is a bank confirmation a highly persuasive type of evidence?

(3)   The minutes of the board of directors meeting mentions three events that occurred in 2013: the continuing construction of the warehouse, the fire damage, and the declaration of a cash dividend. How would each affect the 2012 financial statements? Provide examples of recommended disclosures.

(4)   What is the purpose of a cut-off test? Is the cut-off testing of inventory and sales of significant importance in the Lakeside engagement?

(5)   Mitchell reviewed invoices and cash disbursements in search of any unrecorded liabilities. Why are unrecorded liabilities a special problem for an independent auditor?

(6) Why would the search for contingent losses be a major concern to an auditor?

(7) What information is included on a letter of inquiry mailed to the client's law firm?

(8) Abernethy and Chapman received a letter from the law firm of Benzinger and Dawkins indicating no differences with Lakeside's assessment of contingent losses. Assume that several days later the law firm resigned from any further association with Lakeside. What might this action indicate to the auditing firm and what steps should then be taken?

(9) The case states that a related parties' inquiry letter was sent to the Rogers Development Company. What is the purpose of this document?

(10) According to *Statement of Auditing Standard Number 57*, "Auditing Accounting Estimates," the management of a reporting company must identify the relevant factors that may affect an accounting estimation and then accumulate relevant, sufficient, and reliable information on which to base the estimation. In estimating product warranty liability for 2012, what factors would possibly influence the management's judgment? What information should management use in order to arrive at this estimation?

(11) According to auditing standards, auditors should develop their own independent expectation of an estimate to corroborate the reasonableness of any estimation made by management. For Lakeside's product warranty liability, how should the Abernethy and Chapman auditors go about deriving an independent expectation of the amount?

EXERCISES

(1) Assume that Carole Mitchell has asked you to use the data presented in this case to compute an independent estimation of the accrued product warranty liability as of December 31, 2012. Since this figure will be an estimate, she wants you to prepare an audit document to indicate exactly how the estimation was derived. Also, indicate whether or not the $45,465 figure reported for Accrued Product Warranty is reasonable. Refer to Case 6 for the proper format of audit documents. (Hint: Remember the matching principle!) [Case12.xls]

(2) Prepare the auditor's report that you believe is warranted for the Lakeside Company's 2012 financial statements based on the information contained in the first 11 cases. Lakeside issues comparative financial statements. Assume that any facts not explicitly covered in these cases would not influence the decision as to the type of opinion to be rendered. Be sure to include the reasons why you issued the report that you did. [Case12-2.doc]

APPLY YOUR RESEARCH

Use library resources such as searchable databases to research the following topic.

(1)   One of the procedures Abernethy and Chapman followed in this case is to mail a letter to Lakeside's attorneys concerning litigation, claims, and assessments. Write a report concerning the communication between the auditor and the client's lawyers. What items are communicated? Why is this communication necessary? What is the quality of these types of communications in terms of audit evidence?

CONSULTING PARTNER REVIEW

Bob Zimmerman, the consulting partner on the Lakeside engagement, is concerned about the following issues and would like for you to respond to them. The audio clips are available online at www.prenhall.com/arens.

(1)   The lawyer's letter and contingencies

Exhibit 12-1

Lakeside Company
SUMMARY OF PRODUCT WARRANTY EXPENSE (Prepared by Client)
January, 2011 through December, 2012

MONTH	January 2011	February 2011	March 2011	April 2011
Sales for Month	$1,064,000	$632,000	$718,000	$958,000
Returns:[1]				
Current Month Sales	$386	$274	$354	$444
1 Month Old Sales	$890	$1,066	$776	$658
2 Month Old Sales	$1,198	$1,386	$1,674	$638
3 Month Old Sales	$1,110	$846	$2,574	$1,750
4 Month Old Sales	$1,140	$1,316	$1,972	$2,376
5 Month Old Sales	$656	$578	$1,526	$2,042
6 Month Old Sales	$646	$570	$506	$970
Total	$6,026	$6,036	$9,382	$8,878

MONTH	May 2011	June 2011	July 2011	August 2011
Sales for Month	$972,000	$828,000	$742,000	$920,000
Returns:				
Current Month Sales	$294	$122	$512	$568
1 Month Old Sales	$738	$1,028	$552	$626
2 Month Old Sales	$962	$960	$1,250	$858
3 Month Old Sales	$1,324	$1,316	$1,182	$882
4 Month Old Sales	$686	$640	$912	$1,404
5 Month Old Sales	$1,584	$1,142	$410	$456
6 Month Old Sales	$422	$890	$914	$502
Total	$6,010	$6,098	$5,732	$5,296

MONTH	September 2011	October 2011	November 2011	December 2011
Sales for Month	$884,000	$1,066,000	$1,172,000	$1,600,000
Returns:				
Current Month Sales	$420	$584	$938	$1,010
1 Month Old Sales	$994	$1,118	$1,166	$1,126
2 Month Old Sales	$1,138	$924	$1,258	$1,332
3 Month Old Sales	$1,594	$1,082	$1,278	$1,328
4 Month Old Sales	$2,058	$1,470	$1,024	$1,208
5 Month Old Sales	$1,624	$1,396	$980	$912
6 Month Old Sales	$404	$1,034	$440	$544
Total	$8,232	$7,608	$7,084	$7,460

---

[1]These columns represent actual returns for goods that were sold during the month listed. For example, the $445 listed under January 2011, "1 Month Old Sales," were items sold in December of 2010 and returned in January of 2011.

Exhibit 12-1 (continued)

MONTH	January 2012	February 2012	March 2012	April 2012
Sales for Month	$1,221,000	$762,000	$692,000	$1,114,000
Returns:				
Current Month Sales	$646	$672	$468	$670
1 Month Old Sales	$1,896	$1,938	$732	$702
2 Month Old Sales	$1,314	$1,770	$1,722	$794
3 Month Old Sales	$1,834	$1,690	$2,148	$1,830
4 Month Old Sales	$1,188	$1,250	$1,596	$2,402
5 Month Old Sales	$1,350	$1,398	$1,000	$1,314
6 Month Old Sales	$398	$782	$280	$1,166
Total	$8,626	$9,500	$7,946	$8,878

MONTH	May 2012	June 2012	July 2012	August 2012
Sales for Month	$1,180,000	$818,000	$844,000	$1,100,000
Returns:	$0	$0	$0	$0
Current Month Sales	$842	$736	$1,198	$502
1 Month Old Sales	$1,340	$1,472	$884	$674
2 Month Old Sales	$820	$1,532	$1,368	$1,032
3 Month Old Sales	$1,160	$1,054	$2,108	$1,894
4 Month Old Sales	$2,046	$1,098	$584	$1,436
5 Month Old Sales	$2,020	$1,616	$1,038	$936
6 Month Old Sales	$1,408	$1,390	$970	$610
Total	$9,636	$8,898	$8,150	$7,084

MONTH	September 2012	October 2012	November 2012	December 2012
Sales for Month	$1,022,000	$1,205,000	$1,284,000	$1,748,000
Returns:	$0	$0	$0	$0
Current Month Sales	$554	$440	$846	$1,008
1 Month Old Sales	$1,504	$1,476	$1,538	$1,570
2 Month Old Sales	$750	$2,406	$1,660	$1,868
3 Month Old Sales	$1,328	$1,498	$1,704	$1,752
4 Month Old Sales	$1,788	$1,254	$1,648	$1,204
5 Month Old Sales	$1,150	$1,998	$1,106	$1,048
6 Month Old Sales	$1,288	$1,340	$1,158	$1,032
Total	$8,362	$10,412	$9,660	$9,482

The Lakeside Company: Auditing Cases

13.   CONSULTING AND OTHER SERVICES

Approximately three weeks after completing the 2012 examination of Lakeside Company's financial statements, the CPA firm of Abernethy and Chapman provided a letter to Mr. Frank Markus, chairman of Lakeside's audit committee, and sent a copy to Mr. Rogers, outlining improvements recommended in internal control. Deficiencies noted by the audit team were described along with proposed changes in the design of Lakeside's systems and the various control procedures being utilized. Improvements in internal control and monitoring were considered high priority in light of the question about the initial public offering.

Abernethy and Chapman cited at several points in this lette,r the need to further automate the gathering and reporting of information within the organization. According to the auditors, a large percentage of the data generated by Lakeside has to be hand-recorded onto preprinted forms and then physically routed to the various parties needing the information. Although these procedures had proven adequate when the company was comprised of only two or three stores, recent growth had placed a serious strain on the system's ability to operate effectively. Errors and lost forms were not uncommon; a number of instances had been encountered during the audit where shipments were delayed, incorrect inventory was acquired, and payments were improperly recorded. Service to the company's customers appeared to be hampered by Lakeside's inability to disseminate information quickly and efficiently.

Mr. Markus requested a meeting with Dan Cline, the audit partner, to discuss the letter and some of his own concerns. At that meeting Mr. Markus expressed his concern about what he considered irregular financial reporting. He noted in particular that some of the internal control deficiencies might lead to misleading financial statements. He thought it odd that, while quarterly reports were always a little behind expectations, the year-end report indicated strong growth and a healthy balance sheet.

Shortly after this meeting with Mr. Markus, Dan Cline held a follow-up meeting with the audit team. He wanted to determine whether the audit approach used by the team had maintained sufficient professional skepticism and to explore ways in which the financial statements could be subject to intentional misstatements.

Shortly after receiving this report, Benjamin Rogers, Lakeside's president, telephoned Dan Cline, the audit partner with Abernethy and Chapman. Rogers expressed considerable interest in correcting these deficiencies. He commented that future corporate growth depended on Lakeside's commitment to "continue well into the twenty-first century so that our customers receive the outstanding service that will make them want to buy from us again and again." Following this conversation, Cline asked David Klontz, a consulting services partner with the CPA firm, to contact Rogers and outline the types of technical assistance offered by Abernethy and Chapman. Cline wanted Rogers to know that specialized skills were available within the firm to help Lakeside implement the desired changes in Lakeside's organization. Abernathy and Chapman are also considering the PCAOB rules regarding proscribed services, and have not yet fully implemented new policies to bring themselves in line with these regulations.

Klontz arranged a luncheon meeting with Rogers in order to describe the range of services provided by the firm. During their discussion, Klontz recommended that, as a first step, Lakeside should expand its use of computers to include more terminals at strategic points within the operation. Additional software programs could then be purchased or developed to perform specified operating tasks for the company. In response, Rogers admitted to possessing little knowledge of computer applications. He had previously resisted the expansion of the company's computer facilities because of the enormous difficulties he foresaw in converting to a fully computerized information system. Selecting a new computer, acquiring software, and installing new systems seemed an almost overwhelming chore to Rogers. Just as importantly, he could envision only a few ways in which an enhanced computer system would be adapted to the specific needs of the Lakeside Company. "In the past, I have been very hesitant. I have never understood how the benefits of further computerization could possibly outweigh the many problems and costs involved. Also, will we be able to be as 'hands on' as we have in the past? Will we really know what is going on? However, our growth seems to require that I make changes in the way that I think."

Klontz assured Rogers that the CPA firm would be pleased to investigate Lakeside's needs in detail and then recommend the purchase of a specific computer system. Thereafter, personnel from Abernethy and Chapman would either develop appropriate software for the company or identify outside computer programs to be acquired. The firm was also willing to assist in the installation of all new systems as well as the training of Lakeside employees. According to Klontz, this entire process would create little disturbance within Lakeside's organization. After posing a number of questions about computers and accounting systems, Rogers requested that Klontz prepare a complete proposal to describe possible future actions.

Following this luncheon, Klontz reviewed the entire Lakeside audit documentation file maintained by Abernethy and Chapman. He studied the design of each of the systems that had been analyzed by the audit team. With this understanding of the client's organization and current internal control, he began to write descriptions of the various functions that could be further computerized. The first portion of this list is reproduced in Exhibit 13-1. When completed, Klontz will present these ideas to Rogers as a basis for determining the specific activities that a newly acquired computer system would be designed to accomplish.

DISCUSSION QUESTIONS

(1) During the audit, Abernethy and Chapman apparently uncovered a number of control problems within Lakeside's organization. What action should have been taken if the audit team had discovered a material weakness in the client's internal control?

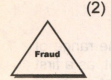

(2) Dan Cline asked the audit team to reconsider their professional skepticism and to evaluate how the financial statements of Lakeside could be subject to manipulation. Using all the previous cases, where has the audit team found evidence of the potential for financial statement manipulation? Is there sufficient evidence of manipulation?

(3) Rogers admits to being hesitant about acquiring and converting to a fully computerized accounting system. Considering the prevalence of computers in today's world, why would a businessperson be so troubled by this action?

(4) Why has the offering of consulting services become so commonplace in public accounting firms? How have recent regulations affected this part of every firm's practice? Can this work continue?

(5) If Lakeside does convert to a completely computerized system, how does this change impact the audit work performed by Abernethy and Chapman in subsequent examinations?

(6) After completing the annual audit, Abernethy and Chapman proposed that the client develop new accounting systems. Thereafter, technical assistance was offered to the client in establishing these same systems. Thus, the firm is in a position to generate revenues as a result of its own recommendations. Does this action constitute a conflict of interests? Discuss this assuming no public offering, and in the case of a public offering.

(7) The public accounting profession is frequently criticized for allowing firms to provide consulting services to audit clients. The assertion is made that independence is lost in two ways by offering such assistance. First, the auditor gains a vested interest in the client, since future financial success is a reflection of the wisdom of the firm's advice. Second, the accounting systems being examined in future years will have been developed or recommended by the auditor's own organization. In both cases the appearance as well as the actual existence of independence is said to be eroded by the firm's dual role. Does providing consulting services to clients threaten the public's faith in the independent auditing profession? Can these services affect the way that the auditor views the relationship with the client? How has the profession dealt with these situations in recent years?

EXERCISES

(1)   In Exhibit 13-1, Klontz has begun to describe the functions that could be further computerized by Lakeside. Using the information provided in the previous cases, complete this memorandum. [Case13-1.doc]

(2)   In a computerized accounting system, the question of maintaining adequate control becomes an important issue because traditional control procedures are not always applicable. Describe the IT control features that should be designed into the client's system. [Case13-2.doc]

APPLY YOUR RESEARCH

Use library resources such as searchable databases to research the following topic.

(1)   In this case, the firm of Abernethy and Chapman was asked to do consulting work for Lakeside that is completely separate and unrelated to the audit of the financial statements. Write a report discussing the potential conflict of interest when an auditor does consulting work for an audit client. Does this relationship cause the independence of the auditor to be violated? Why or why not? Since the Enron debacle, how has the accounting profession dealt with this issue?

CONSULTING PARTNER REVIEW

Bob Zimmerman, the consulting partner on the Lakeside engagement, is concerned about the following issues and would like for you to respond to them. The audio clips are available online at www.prenhall.com/arens.

(1)   Problems associated with consulting for an audit client
(2)   Ensuring that consulting for an audit client is not a problem

THE IMPACT OF SARBANES-OXLEY

(1)   According to Case 1, the Lakeside Company is considering a public offering of stock to finance its growth. At present, Abernethy and Chapman do not presently have any audit clients that are public companies. Write a report discussing how the Sarbannes-Oxley Act impacts the firm's independence regarding the provision of audit and non-audit services.

Exhibit 13-1

Abernethy and Chapman

LAKESIDE COMPANY
FUNCTIONS TO BE FURTHER COMPUTERIZED

Memo Prepared by: David Klontz

(1)   Telephone Sales

Telephone orders are received by an operator in the sales department or electronically via the Internet. Pertinent information for each transaction is entered directly into a computer terminal: client name and address, account number, and the quantity and serial numbers of the items being acquired. The computer verifies the client data against an approved customer file. The specific purchases are then compared to a list of inventory items currently being held in the company's warehouse. The computer indicates to the operator the validity of the client's credit and the availability of the inventory. This information is conveyed immediately over the telephone to the customer with the transaction finalized at that time. The operator either enters approval for the sale or voids the transaction.

(2)   Inventory Shipments

A computerized list of valid sales transactions is maintained in chronological order. Using a terminal, the shipping department requests the next order to be processed. The customer and address are shown on the screen as well as the individual items that have been acquired. Once this merchandise has been packed, the department enters the date of the shipment, the bill of lading number, and the specific inventory being transferred by scanning a bar code. Edit checks are incorporated into the software to verify the shipment data against the order and indicates any items that do not match.